SpringerBriefs in Psychology

For further volumes:
http://www.springer.com/series/10143

Michael Leiter

Analyzing and Theorizing the Dynamics of the Workplace Incivility Crisis

Michael Leiter
CORD
Acadia University
Wolfville
NS, Canada

ISSN 2192-8363 ISSN 2192-8371 (electronic)
ISBN 978-94-007-5570-3 ISBN 978-94-007-5571-0 (eBook)
DOI 10.1007/978-94-007-5571-0
Springer Dordrecht Heidelberg New York London

Library of Congress Control Number: 2012948465

Printed on acid-free paper

Springer is part of Springer Science+Business Media (www.springer.com)

Contents

Chapter 1
The Current Crisis

Abstract Workplace mistreatment has emerged as a compelling social concern at the beginning of the twenty-first century. A Risk Management Model provides a context for understanding the roots of workplace incivility, the extent of its emotional impact, and its downstream consequences. The chapter introduces the model that focuses on people within the context of a social environment, the climate of which has momentum for remaining constant over time. The model leads to propositions for designing interventions to improve the quality of work-life. This chapter provides an overview of the book, introducing constructs that will be explored in greater depth in subsequent chapters.

Incivility as a Contemporary Workplace Crisis

People are having a hard time getting along with one another these days. Workplaces from preschools to hospices resonate with complaints about bullying, incivility, and aggression. Otherwise reasonable professionals to whom much is given and from whom much is expected neglect core responsibilities while sinking into petty disputes with their colleagues.

These incidents are more than unfortunate lapses of good manners. They work their way into defining the culture of a workplace. Employees' mistreatment of one another takes various forms—bullying, abuse, aggression, conflict, mobbing, social undermining, and incivility—but they all share expressions of disrespect among people responsible for working together. This book focuses on incivility as the entry level form of workplace mistreatment. Andersson and Pearson (1999) defined workplace incivility as "low intensity deviant behavior with ambiguous intent to harm the target, in violation of workplace norms for mutual respect. Uncivil behaviors are characteristically rude and discourteous, displaying a lack of

M. Leiter, *Analyzing and Theorizing the Dynamics of the Workplace Incivility Crisis*, SpringerBriefs in Psychology,
DOI: 10.1007/978-94-007-5571-0_1,

regard for others" (p. 457). From this definition, the first feature of incivility is low intensity: rude facial expressions and sarcasm rather than screams. Second, it is not always clear whether the other person intended to be rude or to deliberately show disrespect. Incivility may reflect thoughtlessness more than aggression.

Despite its low intensity, incivility has an insidious impact, even when it appears fairly mild on the surface. People don't just shrug it off. People on whom clients depend for informed if not courageous action feel helpless when meeting scorn from their colleagues or bosses. With so many far-reaching ramifications, the challenge of reducing incivility while increasing the overall level of workplace civility has become a priority of major proportions. It needs action now.

Exploring the social and personal context of incivility sheds light on fundamental questions within psychology.

- Why do people behave badly towards colleagues at work? From what perspective does this behavior make sense?
- Why does it matter? Why do people care so much about others behaving badly towards them?
  - Why do people find bullying to be so emotionally devastating?
  - Why do subtle instances of incivility and disrespect have such a powerful impact?
- Most importantly: What can be done about it? How can individuals or organizations improve the level of civility in their worksetting, including:
  - Individual Strategies
  - Group Strategies
  - Organizational Strategies.

These questions touch upon fundamental issues about people and their relationships with others. For some, they have implications for personal identity. Relationships are an important part of identity, and experiencing a relationship breakdown challenges identity to some extent. Addressing these issues can open opportunities for career development; failing to address them can shut down opportunities entirely. The answers determine the extent to which people can develop a sense of community at work.

For organizations the quality of working relationships has implications for productivity as well as the quality of worklife. Improving civility in day-to-day encounters among employees provides a route to greater engagement of employees in their work.

Conceptual Framework

A Risk Management Model of workplace mistreatment provides a way to approach these questions. It starts from the idea that people are both delightful and dangerous. This range of possibilities leads to uncertainty: which quality will describe the next social encounter? Much can be gained or lost. Managing the inherent risks presents a fundamental life challenge. A conservative strategy of minimal involvement safeguards against harm, but has serious costs when it causes one to miss opportunities for pleasant, constructive involvement. A libertine strategy of enthusiastic immersion maximizes opportunities but may result in emotional harm. Further, in today's multi-faceted work world, people can be overwhelmed by too many commitments. A necessary life skill is maintaining a balance that contains risk while giving access to opportunities. The level of civility and respect within a workplace culture provides essential information for maintaining such a balance.

The following section provides a broad overview of the Risk Management Model's main components. Subsequent sections and chapters expand on these constructs, placing them within recent research and theory development in this field. The final chapters consider the Model's implications for workplace intervention and management practice.

The Risk Management Model of workplace civility proposes that people continually monitor the potential risks in their social environment. This monitoring occurs because (1) one's place in the social environment is important and (2) people are capable of assessing the situation. These considerations lead to the first two propositions of the Risk Management Model:

Proposition 1: People want to Belong

People are Motivated to have Good Standing Within a Social Group

Thriving in the contemporary world requires reasonable connections with others. Being perceived as an effective team player is an asset. Social standing in a workgroup is a worthy focus of that precious and limited resource: one's attention. The importance of social monitoring is not new. From an evolutionary perspective, community membership was essential in early history when the tribe was vital for individuals to survive threats to their physical safety. Community membership remains of vital importance in the contemporary world of global social networks, interdependent economic systems, and interdisciplinary teamwork.

Proposition 2: People Notice

People have a Refined Perception of Social Cues and a Capacity to Make Sense of Social Situations

Monitoring is important because one's good standing in a community is essential for career development and economic wellbeing. Monitoring is feasible because people have a refined sensitivity to subtle social cues. Individuals effortlessly read signals of relative status into the gestures, word choice, and intonation of those with whom they interact. Seeing oneself as others see you is a survival skill. Participants conclude from brief exchanges the extent to which others consider them respectable, inconsequential, or worthy of scorn. Some cues are inherent in a national culture, such as the firmness of a handshake or the depth of a bow. Other cues may be specific to an organization or a workgroup, such as an invitation to lunch or a public rebuke. Certain cues, such as a welcoming smile, may be universal. Some are enduing while other cues shift with the fashions of the times. Despite the subtlety, complexity, and changing nature of social cues, people learn to recognize and interpret them. It's something at which most, although not all, people are adept.

The social world is fraught with peril, but these perils are manageable to some extent. Recognizing its importance, people are motivated to monitor their environment to identify hazards and take appropriate action to reduce identified risks. Workplace civility communicates a low level of risk. Behaving civilly towards someone acknowledges the other person as deserving of respect as a member of a shared community. In contrast, workplace incivility signals increased riskiness in the workplace environment. Incivility, whether directed towards oneself or towards others, signals that community membership can be revoked. In a dangerous world, civility conveys safety; incivility conveys risk. As actions exclude a person from a community, they weaken an individual's capacity to thrive. Being excluded from a community weakens a person's coping resources because belonging to a community provides many options for managing demands. Exclusion leaves targets with fewer people to call upon for instrumental or emotional support. The strong connection of incivility with social standing strengthens the emotional impact of incivility at work.

Although incivility by definition has low intensity in itself, its implications can be far reaching. In the most immediate sense, by bending the rules of comportment, acts of incivility weaken expectations for reasonable professional discourse among members of a workgroup. Rude comments introduce doubts about the perpetrators, for example, that they lack the self-management qualities necessary to maintain composure. It may as well introduce doubts about management's commitment to supporting the values of a respectful workplace: when uncivil behavior is overlooked, relevant organizational values appear as empty statements. These empty statements would fall within Argyris and Schön's (1974) domain of espoused values that are not translated into values-in-action. A weak commitment to espoused values reduces members' confidence that management will actively support this value or any other organizational value subsequently. The situation of empty value statements reduces employees' initiative by increasing risk. For example, a first line manager who observes senior management overlooking workplace incivility or bullying would hesitate before addressing such behavior within her workgroup. Addressing relationship problems presents risks in that employees may bring a grievance against the intervening supervisor or retaliate in other ways. Confidence in management support for enforcing core values would reduce the supervisor's perceived risk, thus increasing the chances of taking action. Without that confidence, the potential negative consequences of taking action appear prohibitively risky.

Incivility worsens the demand/resource balance at work. Incivility in itself makes demands on people. Incivility's demands do not further the mission at work; responding to those demands simply brings conditions back to a steady state. Incivility limits resource access by introducing barriers between individuals. People not only reduce their interactions with people who instigate incivility, they may reduce their level of social interaction more generally. The overall result is a worse balance of resources with demands, a condition that pushes towards burnout and away from work engagement (Demerouti et al. 2001; Maslach and Leiter 1997).

Proposition 3: Workgroup Climates are Self-Perpetuating

A negative emotional tone can be established quickly. It can even occur accidently because intent is not essential to incivility. Once an emotional tone becomes established, it continues. One person can say something—or neglect to say something—without any intent to offend, but offend nonetheless. The Risk Management Model proposes two processes that give momentum to the emotional tone of social encounters among members of workgroups. One process is reciprocity: people give what they receive. If they feel offended, they feel inclined to offend in return. The second process, emotional contagion, operates more broadly, spreading the emotional tone among people who are not directly participating in the exchange. The momentum in emotional exchange maintains the status quo, inhibiting efforts for change. As discussed more extensively in a subsequent section, both of these processes lack reflection. Overcoming this momentum requires a deliberate and effortful act. The energy, courage, or insight needed to take such action is missing in many situations. When the environment appears risky, it makes sense to be cautious.

The increased perceived risk arising from workplace incivility has implications for employees' sense of fairness. Supervisor incivility undermines interactional justice (Bies 2001) by definition with dire implications for distributive or procedural justice. Coworker incivility also undermines interactional justice when it goes unaddressed. The overall impact is an erosion of management trust. Without confidence that management is sincere in its ideals, thorough in applying policies and procedures, and respectful in its encounters with employees, definitive action is risky for employees. The chain of events that would follow employee initiative is shrouded in uncertainty. Individuals cannot project whether management will support them, ignore them, or condemn them when they take initiative in pursuing the organizational mission. For many, the safer alternative is to avoid initiative.

From a personal perspective, incivility also increases the risk of an identity crisis. To the extent identity rests upon working relationships and roles, uncivil interactions present a challenge. Incivility challenges the viability and salience of working relationships. Incivility implies that one is less than one previously believed, presenting a risk to identity. This risk increases the intensity of responses to workplace incivility. As risks increase, trust diminishes.

This book explores the Risk Management Model to consider the prevalence of incivility among members of workgroups and its impact upon their wellbeing and productivity. It builds upon this overview to consider approaches for improving workplace civility.

Mechanisms and Influence

The following section elaborates on mechanisms of the Risk Management Model. These concepts describe the means through which the motivational and sense making qualities that people bring to their social encounters influence their emotional states, their understanding, and their action.

Uncertainty and Risk

The Risk Management Model works from the view that the social environment of an organization is fraught with uncertainty. Social relationships have both emotional and rational qualities. The balance of these two qualities varies with context. Generally, personal relationships—friendships, romance, family—have strong emotional qualities in contrast to professional relationships that have a stronger cognitive component. Professional relationships have a defined goal and are often time-limited in contrast to personal relationships that are more open-ended and non-utilitarian. Incivility in working relationships brings an unwanted and unpleasant emotional quality to collegiality. By moving the relationship out of the rational domain of professional discourse, incivility introduces an element of risk: the parties are uncertain as to how the relationship will develop. It is difficult to know the appropriate response to incivility: should one ignore it, suffer in silence, voice a complaint, reciprocate, or leave the group?

People may create a narrative to make sense of difficult relationships at work. A narrative structure simplifies a complex situation. By drawing upon set roles, such as persecutor, victim, and rescuer triangle (Chefetz 1997), a narrative cuts through the ambiguity of the actual situation. Ideally, a narrative points towards ways in which the situation may resolve. In a parallel way Taffler and Tuckett (2010) describe the use of narrative to make sense of complex financial markets. In contrast to rational economic models, they propose that emotions associated with narrative story lines shape behavior and decisions. Although commonly used narrative forms, such as rags to riches, make only a trivial contribution in comparison with objective data on financial markets, they help people to manage the anxiety that arises when making consequential decisions without complete information. In a parallel fashion, the Risk Management Model proposes that people draw upon narratives to make sense of the complex emotional experience of workplace incivility. Explaining the experience within a simple narrative alleviates anxiety, giving a sense of control. Unfortunately, the narrative rarely contributes to resolution. Social interactions at work rarely follow the simplicity of the narrative structure.

Incivility increases the uncertainty and risk that people experience in a relationship. Expressing incivility towards a colleague violates a constraint on proper behavior. When people operate within agreed-upon rules of comportment, the probabilities seem high that they will continue to do so. Once that line is crossed, it seems increasingly likely that it will be crossed again through further incivility or other disturbing, deviant behavior. Although the incident may be excused as a momentary slip in the perpetrator's self-management, it still demonstrates that such slips have happened and could happen again.

Identity

Another element of the conceptual model contends that part of incivility's impact comes from its implicit challenge to identity. Workplace civility relates to identity in two ways. One pertains to the extent to which people define who they are in terms of their relationships—being someone's son or spouse or coworker or neighbor. At work, key relationships can be defined in terms of work roles—the vice president's executive assistant—or personal relationships—Betty's best friend or Wilbur's bête noire. The work roles and personal relationships together contribute to the way people perceive themselves as well as how others perceive them.

The second way identity relates to civility falls within the domain of Social Identity Theory (SIT; Ashforth and Mael 1989) that considers the processes through which individuals identify with their organization, its subgroups, and its informal groups. SIT concerns the question of identification with a group as distinct from the emotional charge, positive or negative, towards that group. "Identification is the perception of oneness with or belongingness to a group, involving direct or vicarious experience of its successes and failures" (p. 34). The compelling feature of groups that make some of them attractive points of identification is that they are distinctive, prestigious, and in competition with other groups. Belonging to some groups is preferable to belonging to others. Being excluded from highly desirable groups reduces one's status within the organization, thereby increasing risk of further resource loss. Interactions that confirm one's identity in such groups provide a sense of safety.

The general theme is that interactions across the boundaries between identity groups are more contentious than those among members within an identity group. Tajfel (1974) introduced the role of group membership in defining social identity. His argument was that the existence of any identifiable group within an organization was sufficient to establish an in-group/out-group dynamic. His work established that even basing group membership explicitly upon random assignment would engender intergroup boundaries. Interactions across those boundaries differ from those occurring among members within the boundary. Each type of interaction may have its distinct rules to define civility and incivility. It may be that constraints on displaying incivility may be looser for interactions that cross boundaries than for interactions with group members. In any case, Tajfel's work demonstrated that in-group membership had an adverse impact on the quality of interactions with outsiders regardless of whether the parties had a history of problems or the groups were in competition.

The Risk Management Model proposes that incivility poses a social identity threat. Specifically, day-to-day interactions among people at work confirm or challenge an individual's social identity. People monitor the social cues in their interactions to determine how others view their social identities. Signs of disrespect challenge one's identity. For example, in a study of engineering students, Logel et al. (2009) found that women's performance on engineering tasks was adversely affected after interactions that included behavior that reflected sexist attitudes towards women as engineers. This study linked the general concept of group identity with the specific uncivil behaviors that express challenges to identity. Mistreatment at work defines its targets as being unworthy of respect and therefore denies the targets' legitimate standing in the workplace community.

A pervasive quality of incivility is that it challenges its target's identity. Disrespect conveys an implicit message that the person expressing incivility challenges the target's status as a person deserving respect. Even when the perpetrator has no deliberate intention of belittling the other, an unfavorable comment can convey an implicit rejection of the other's identity as a valuable member of the workgroup, a personal friend, or other important role. Through their capacity to undermine identity, these interactions erode the role structure of workplaces. Challenges to identity, especially those from authority figures, have the potential to undermine the targets' capacity to perform (Logel et al. 2009) or to prompt targets to become rigidly defensive in their interactions with others at work. Neither reaction will further the workgroup's level of performance.

Incivility undermines social identity by redefining the target negatively. Simply ignoring someone implies that they are not sufficiently important to warrant attention. Many forms of incivility explicitly demean the other person through direct criticism, mocking, or sarcasm. The interaction not only redefines the relationship of the target with the perpetrator, but also redefines both parties to their colleagues who witness the exchange. The social dimensions of identity become stronger when others concur; they become shaky when identity is challenged, especially when challenged publicly among colleagues.

The Integral Role of Justice in Civility

Challenges to identity become especially distressing when they feel unjust. It may seem tolerable if the CEO is condescending but irritating when a colleague behaves in this way. The relative status of the parties contributes to whether the exchange feels unfair. As Toru Okada in Murakami (1998) novel reflected on father-in-law, "He bowed to superior authority without question, and he trampled those beneath him without hesitation" (p. 48). When one accepts power hierarchies, the idea of fair treatment adapts to the relative status of the participants.

Incivility violates norms of interactional justice that are the standards of reasonable, polite treatment among people within a social setting. Bies (2001) identified four forms of interactional justice: derogatory judgments, deception, privacy invasion, and disrespect. While the work on interactional justice focuses primarily on employees' interactions with managers as purveyors of organizational values and legitimacy (Bies and Shapiro 1987; Laschinger and Finegan 2005), uncivil encounters with colleagues also prompt feelings on injustice.

Feelings of injustice contribute to perpetuating incivility in work settings as people reciprocate or escalate exchanges. The experience of injustice can prompt desire to exact revenge to reciprocate the derogatory nature of an exchange (Barclay et al. 2005). In the course of restoring balance in their relationships with offending colleagues, people are likely to engage in deviant behavior that runs contrary to organizational values and undermines the quality of team functioning. A negative reciprocity norm perpetuates and can even exacerbate an already unfortunate situation.

Unfair treatment from supervisors or managers has the additional impact of diminishing employees' hopes for the future. Even a single incident of supervisor incivility can be sufficient to engender a career crisis. Health care employees who experience one or more instances of supervisor incivility over the previous year were more likely to evaluate their careers as turning out badly (Leiter 2011, November) in contrast to their colleagues who had experienced no supervisor incivility. This effect was more powerful for older health care providers (i. e., Baby Boomers) than for their younger colleagues (Generation X and Millennials). It may be that older health care providers expect a more egalitarian relationship with their supervisors (who are generally their age or younger). Uncivil treatment conveys a more authoritarian attitude with a greater power difference. This type of supervisory relationship may be tolerable for young health care providers while establishing their careers, but for older colleagues it could signal that they have little hope for career development within their current environment. The complex challenge to identity and justice inherent in supervisory incivility may contribute to its powerful emotional impact.

Sharing Experiences: Emotional Contagion and Empathy

Incivility grows in importance as it goes beyond an occasional encounter to pervading a community. The current crisis is more than people occasionally making rude remarks. Breakdowns occur when incivility becomes a regular feature of a workgroup' social climate. Addressing these challenges requires much more than improving the comportment of one or two employees. It requires understanding

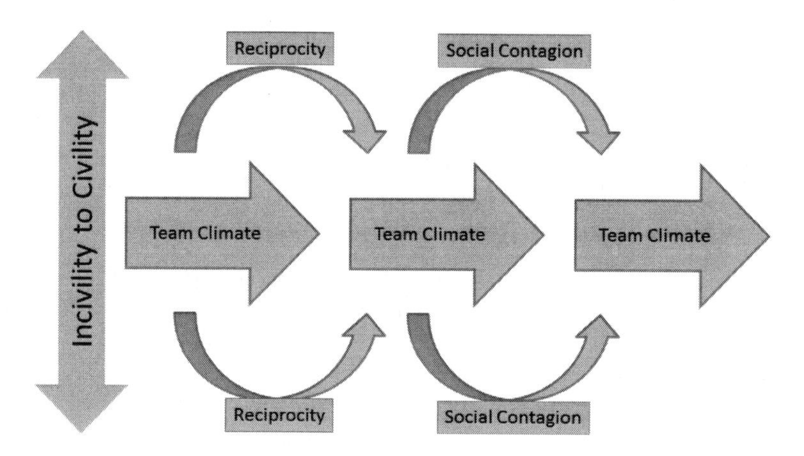

Fig. 1.1 Self-perpetuating processes

the dynamics that perpetuate an unpleasant social dynamic to find a means of intervening effectively (Fig. 1.1).

A powerful dynamic within the Risk Management Model is that people respond to what they receive. Much of social behavior reflects reciprocity: kindness prompts kindness in return; rudeness prompts rudeness. To some extent reciprocity operates on social contagion (Hatfield et al. 1994). Social behavior conveys an emotional tone. When interacting with someone who is displaying a clear emotion, people readily adopt a similar emotional tone. Contagion occurs through mimicking, often outside of awareness, one another's gestures, expressions, or vocal tone, demonstrating a capacity for people to resonate with one another's emotional state.

It may be that one reason that reciprocity has such a pervasive presence in social interactions is that people automatically mimic and mirror one another's emotionally charged behavior. When approached by a smiling colleague, people readily return the smile, increasing the likelihood of positive emotions. When approached by an angry or dismissive colleague, the cues prompt anger or defensiveness. The ease with which people resonate with one another's emotions opens people to influence from non-rational sources. They may then behave in ways that are inconsistent with their professional role and responsibilities at work.

Coplan (2011) distinguishes emotional contagion from empathy, describing emotional contagion as a reflexive response to others' emotional state independent of thoughtful consideration. That is, an observer can share a target's fear on the basis of observing gestures, facial expressions, and behavior that express fear without any consideration of why the target is fearful. In contrast, empathy requires deliberate, conscious understanding of the target's perspective. To be empathic requires the observer to not only know how the target feels, but to comprehend the basis of that feeling as well. She supports her argument with neuroscience research (Singer 2006; Singer and Lamm 2009) demonstrating that emotional contagion is closely involved with the limbic system while empathy requires active involvement of prefrontal and temporal cortex. As such, empathy is a higher order cognitive process requiring greater concentration and mental effort from people than does participating in emotional contagion. Coplan goes further in distinguishing self and other oriented empathy, labelling the self-oriented variety as pseudo-empathy, because it relies excessively on an egocentric bias. That is, pseudo-empathy builds on a projection process—if I were in that situation, I would feel X—that assumes that the observer and target are alike. This assumption is viable to the extent that two people are identical or that they are in situations, such as an attack by a ferocious animal, that prompt universal reactions. This assumption is tenuous at best in the complex, multicultural, multidisciplinary, multigenerational work world of the twenty-first century. People encounter others who differ from them in ways that shape the others' emotional reactions to a variety of situations. For examples, incidents such as hearing off-color jokes that are trivial to one person may be deeply offensive if not frightening to another. For both parties, imagining how they would react in this situation would fall well short of empathy with the other.

Additionally, it is difficult at times to identify the issues that are salient to the other person's emotional reaction. Contemporary workplaces present people with a diverse range of complex situations. For example, in a department meeting, the supervisor criticizes an individual for arriving late. One employee feels smug because she is confident in her punctuality; another employee is fearful because the boss's decision to embarrass a fellow employee publicly suggests a risk of further such reprimands. Complex situations can prompt a wide variety of responses from people. No one has perfect information about complex organizational developments. Various stakeholders hold different bits of incomplete information, elements of which may be supporting their interests while other elements may be contradicting their interests. The boss may be solely concerned with punctuality or the boss may be embarking on a crusade to shape up employee behavior overall. It's unlikely that even people with similar values would react identically to the dilemmas and changes in their worklife. A central message of Coplan (2011) is that these variations in emotional resonance among people are not simply a matter of degree and intensity. Emotional contagion, pseudo-empathy, and empathy occupy qualitatively distinct domains. They differ in their antecedents, their consequences, and their underlying neural and psychological processes.

The Risk Management Model proposes that emotional contagion sustains a workgroup climate. Specific encounters have an emotional tone that influences the broader social discourse within the workgroup. Emotional contagion has a direct impact among people who are participating in an encounter as well as an indirect impact on others in proximity (Davies 2011; Hatfield et al. 1994). Emotional contagion provides a mechanism through which incivility has an impact on observers who are not directly participating in a specific encounter (Andersson and Pearson 1999). The encounter not only offends their sense of propriety or fair play, but conveys the emotional tone of the person taking offense. In situations of intended incivility, there may be additional emotional qualities associated with aggression or disrespect. When the emotional tone is supportive, emotional contagion helps to sustain that quality; when the emotional tone is aggressive or disdainful, it perpetuates an unpleasant workplace.

Improving Workplace Communities

One objective of this book is to explore the contribution of the Risk Management Model to improving workplace communities. The self-perpetuating quality of workplace cultures call for definitive action to interrupt their momentum to establish more civil respectful discourse. The following section presents two core propositions that receive elaboration in Chaps. 4, 5, and 6.

Proposition 4: Improving Civility Benefits from Psychological Safety

Proposition 5: Improving Civility Requires a Reflective Process

The Risk Management Model proposes that empathy contributes to improving workplace culture. Empathy works quite differently from emotional contagion. Rather than perpetuating emotionally charged workplace dynamics, empathy introduces two qualities that interrupt that flow.

First, empathy has a clear separation of self and other. Coplan (2011) emphasizes this point in contrasting empathy and pseudo-empathy that is built upon the question: what would I feel like in that situation. Pseudo-empathy softens the boundary between the observer and the target, minimizing differences in their experiences, cultural backgrounds, and values. It works from the assumption that everyone shares my values and attitudes. True empathy presents a greater challenge of considering a situation from the perspective of someone with a different point of view. Perspective taking of this sort makes demands upon intelligence, imagination, and concentration. It requires people to move from the less energy-intensive mode of egocentric thinking to testing a more generous perspective on the people around one. As Coplan (2011) notes, "empathy is a motivated and controlled process, which is neither automatic nor involuntary and demands that the observer attend to relevant differences between self and other" (p. 58–59). It requires observers to think from an unfamiliar and perhaps uncomfortable point of view, to control their automatic emotional responses to a situation, and to know something about the target of their empathy (Goldie 2002). The operation of a controlled process interferes with the smooth unfolding of automatic, subconscious processes, such as emotional contagion, that perpetuate existing dynamics.

Second, empathy requires a concern for the target's experience. The effort and concentration required to move away from an egocentric perspective imply an active consideration of the target. The observers' emotional experience overlaps somewhat with that of the target, but differs in that the observer also has a reaction to the target's experience. For example, when empathizing with a colleague experiencing distress after being publicly criticized by her boss, the observer registers the target's emotional distress supplemented by a direct emotional experience that may include anger, pity, or bewilderment. The introduction of this direct emotional experience of the observer helps to move the situation away from an automatic response.

As such, empathy in itself increases the possibility of a group establishing a new mode of interacting with one another. When emotional contagion dominates interactions among people, then the current state perpetuates itself without reflection. People respond to anger with anger and to condescension with resentment. If all is going well, a group may have the pleasure of maintaining a pleasant, respectful mode of interaction effortlessly, without reflection. However, when disrespect and incivility occur, the dynamic becomes self-perpetuating. The situation may even spiral into ever-increasing unpleasantness (Pearson et al. 2005). The compelling nature of emotional contagion would likely prompt reactions that would maintain the existing emotional tone. The distinct qualities of empathy recommend it to play a central role in designing interventions to improve workplace civility.

An Integrative Model

The Risk Management Model integrates constructs that have emerged across research and theory development on job burnout, work engagement, and workplace mistreatment. The model has many inter-connected elements. In a parallel fashion, a workgroup's social network comprises myriad distinct social encounters among its members. Each of these encounters has a quality that can range from offensive incivility to genteel civility. That quality both reflects the state of the core elements (social contagion, empathy, identity, justice, and uncertainty) and influences in turn the future state of those elements.

The Risk Management Model proposes that civility mediates the relationship of these elements with key outcomes. For example, both cynicism on the Maslach Burnout Inventory General Scale (Maslach et al. 1996) and fairness from the Areas of Worklife Scale (Leiter and Maslach 2004 have strong correlations with psychological safety (Edmondson 1999). The Model proposes that the level of civility in collegial social encounters will mediate these relationships. Specifically, after entering civility in the first step of the regression on psychological safety, the relationship of cynicism or fairness will be significantly smaller than the base correlation.

This aspect of the model defines an active role for civility. It is not simply an outcome to predict or another factor to predict organizational or personal outcomes. Instead, civility provides the medium through which personal attitudes or management policies have an impact on people. The quality of civility or incivility in workplace encounters is that people bring a capacity for communicating nuanced views on their relationships through their social behavior and the targets of these behaviors have the capacity to interpret these signals. The dynamics become especially complex because the person initiating the encounter may communicate more than was intended through subconscious facial expressions or other behaviors.

As such, workplace civility provides a rich source of information on worklife. As a somewhat but not completely consciously controlled part of life, it has a great potential to benefit from intervention. As suggested by the discussion of empathy, the capacity to interrupt the flow of exchange through focused, deliberate action that appreciates a clear distinct between the observer and the target has the potential to change working relationships for the better.

The Structure of this Book

Chapter 2 reviews research on the prevalence and impact of workplace incivility. It puts incivility in context of more intense forms of workplace mistreatment: bullying, aggression, and abuse.

Chapter 3 reviews research on the determinants of workplace incivility. It considers the personal, group, organizational, and cultural factors that contribute to workplace civility and incivility.

Chapter 4 develops the Risk Management model to consider its implications for developing interventions to improve workplace civility.

Chapter 5 presents an organizational intervention to improve civility (CREW) that has been implemented throughout the Veterans Health Administration in the USA.

Chapter 6 presents perspectives on the Risk Management Model from research on CREW conducted in Canadian hospitals.

Chapter 7 integrates these elements into a framework for considering workplace civility.

References

Andersson, L. M., & Pearson, C. M. (1999). Tit for tat? The spiraling effect of incivility in the workplace. *The Academy of Management Review, 24*, 452–471.

Argyris, C., & Schön, D. A. (1974). *Theory in practice, increasing professional effectiveness*. San Francisco: Jossey-Bass.

Ashforth, B. E., & Mael, F. (1989). Social identity theory and the organization. *The Academy of Management Review, 14*, 20–39.

Barclay, L. J., Skarlicki, D. P., & Pugh, S. D. (2005). Exploring the role of emotions in injustice perceptions and retaliation. *Journal of Applied Psychology, 90*, 629–643.

Bies, R. J. (2001). Interactional (in)justice: The sacred and the profane. In J. Greenberg & R. Cropanzano (Eds.), *Advances in organizational justice* (pp. 89–118). Stanford: Stanford University Press.

Bies, R. J., & Shapiro, D. L. (1987). Interactional fairness judgments: The influence of causal accounts. *Social Justice Research, 1*, 199–218.

Chefetz, R. A. (1997). Special case transferences and counter transferences in the treatment of dissociative disorders. *Dissociation, 10*(4), 255–265.

Coplan, A. (2011). Will the real empathy please stand up? A case for a narrow conceptualization. *The Southern Journal of Philosophy, 49*, 40–65.

Davies, S. (2011). Infectious music: Music-listener emotional contagion. In P. Goldie & A. Coplan (Eds.), *Empathy: Philosophical and psychological perspectives*. Oxford: Oxford University Press.

Demerouti, E., Bakker, A. B., Nachreiner, F., & Schaufeli, W. B. (2001). The job demands-resources model of burnout. *Journal of Applied Psychology, 86*, 499–512.

Edmondson, A. (1999). Psychological safety and learning behavior in work teams. *Administrative Science Quarterly, 44*, 350–383.

Goldie, P. (2002). *The emotions: A philosophical exploration*. Oxford: Oxford University Press.

Hatfield, E., Cacioppo, J. T., & Rapson, R. L. (1994). *Emotional contagion: Studies in emotion and social interaction*. Cambridge: Cambridge University Press.

Laschinger, H. K. S., & Finegan, J. E. (2005). Using empowerment to build trust and respect in the workplace: A strategy for addressing the nursing shortage. *Nursing Economics, 23*, 6–13.

Leiter, M. P. (2011, November). *Distinct implications of career evaluations across generations: Implications of workplace civility. Presentation at the Conference: Age Cohorts in the Workforce*. Trento, Italy.

Leiter, M. P., & Maslach, C. (2004). Areas of worklife: A structured approach to organizational predictors of job burnout. In P. Perrewé & D. C. Ganster (Eds.), Research in occupational stress and well-being. *Emotional and physiological processes and positive intervention strategies* (Vol. 3, pp. 91–134). Oxford: JAI Press/Elsevier.

Logel, C., Walton, G. M., Spencer, S. J., Iserman, E. C., von Hippel, W., & Bell, A. (2009). Interacting with sexist men triggers social identity threat among female engineers. *Journal of Personality and Social Psychology, 96*, 1089–1103.

Maslach, C., Jackson, S. E., & Leiter, M. P. (1996). *Maslach burnout inventory manual* (3rd ed.). Palo Alto: Consulting Psychologists Press.

Maslach, C., & Leiter, M. P. (1997). *The truth about burnout*. San Francisco: Jossey Bass.

Murakami, H. (1998). *The wind-up bird chronicle*. New York: Vintage.

Pearson, C., Andersson, L., & Porath, C. (2005). Workplace incivility. In S. Fox & P. E. Spector (Eds.), *Counterproductive work behavior: Investigations of actors and targets*. Washington: American Psychological Association.

Singer, T. (2006). The neuronal basis and ontogeny of empathy and mind reading: Review of literature and implications for future research. *Neuroscience and Biobehavioral Reviews, 30*, 855–863.

Singer, T., & Lamm, C. (2009). The social neuroscience of empathy. *Annals of the New York Academy of Science, 1156*, 81–89.

Taffler, R. J., & Tuckett, D. A. (2010). Emotional finance: The role of the unconscious in financial decisions. In H. K. Baker & J. R. Nofsinger (Eds.), *Behavioral finance: Investors, corporations, and markets* (pp. 95–114). New York: Wiley.

Tajfel, H. (1974). Social identity and intergroup behavior. *Social Science Information/sur les sciences sociales, 13*, 65–93.

Chapter 2
Forms of Workplace Mistreatment

Abstract This chapter explores the definitions of various forms of workplace mistreatment, contrasting them with a definition of workplace incivility. The chapter considers conceptual models for understanding the causes, processes, and consequences of workplace mistreatment, indicating the potential contribution of the Risk Management Model. A section towards the end of the chapter reflects upon the first two propositions introduced in Chap. 1 regarding the importance of belonging as a motive and the human capacity to perceive and interpret their social world.

Definitions and Implications of Incivility

What is Incivility?

The ways in which people mistreat one another at work has attracted concern from managers, consultants, professional groups, and academics over recent decades. This interest has brought an important issue well-deserved attention. Extensive surveys across a variety of occupational groups have established that workplace mistreatment occurs entirely too often. Large scale surveys report diverse rates of workplace bullying, ranging from 5 to 50 % (Zapf et al. 2003). A regional survey in the south of France found that 10 % of participants had experienced workplace bullying and that the experience of bullying was associated with sleep disturbances (Niedhammer et al. 2000). Schat et al. (2006) found that 6 % of participants in a national survey in the USA reported workplace violence while 41.4 % reported psychological aggression. Bullying towards nurses occurs so frequently that nurses consider it a normal part of the nursing profession (Advisory Board Company 2009; Hutchinson et al. 2005). Surveys have reported that 21 % of USA employees have been the target of workplace bullying (Keashly and Jagatic 2000; Namie and

M. Leiter, *Analyzing and Theorizing the Dynamics of the Workplace Incivility Crisis*, SpringerBriefs in Psychology,
DOI: 10.1007/978-94-007-5571-0_2,

Namie 2000). The exact figures vary with working populations and definitions of mistreatment, but it leads to a consensus that these things occur too frequently.

Yamada (2000) defined bullying as "the intentional infliction of a hostile work environment upon an employee by a coworker or coworkers, typically through a combination of verbal and nonverbal behaviors" (p. 480). Namie and Namie (2007) defined it as "repeated mistreatment by one or more perpetrators of an individual or group… driven by a need to control other people" (p. 43). Keashly (1998) defined bullying as "hostile verbal and nonverbal, nonphysical behaviors directed at a person(s) such that the target's sense of him/herself as a competent person and worker is negatively affected" (p. 86). Whatever may be the ideal definition for bullying, it comprises unpleasant, unwanted social behavior that has no constructive place in workplace cultures.

The Broader Context of Incivility

Mistreatment of colleagues at work occurs within a broader context of a civility crisis. Workplaces are one of many venues for incivility. People complain of receiving or witnessing frequent incivility while driving, going to school, walking on the sidewalk, and participating in the political process. They see incivility in a diminished use of *please* and *thank you*, abrupt interruptions from communication technologies, people using public space as if it were their own personal space, diminished concerned for community, and blatant shows of disrespect for leaders (Alkon 2010; Mills 2012; Truss 2005). The incivility crisis has been attributed to a clash of cultures: people from differing national backgrounds encountering one another more frequently in a global community (Morand 2003). In a parallel manner, clashing codes of comportment across generations result in older people dismissing young people as rude, uncultured louts lacking a work ethic (Leiter et al. 2010). Mills (2012) emphasized the importance of distinguishing discussions of societal and personal civility. Stereotypical thinking occurs at the intersections of cultures as people from one culture apply their views of comportment to people from another. This situation differs in a meaningful way from within-culture incivility that may arise from either (1) perpetrators who have failed to learn proper comportment or (2) perpetrators who choose to violate civility despite knowing proper comportment. Ideally, people would learn and exercise codes of civility as they pertain to each person they encounter, adapting their own behavior to accommodate the feelings of the other. Regardless of whether attaining such an ideal is possible, it does not appear likely in the foreseeable future.

Alkon (2010) opens her book referring to invasions of public space by people talking loudly on phones. A bygone era contained telephone calls in phone booths; now phone conversations are ubiquitous. The loud and generally vapid conversation invades the mental space of neighboring people. Conversation tends to attract attention even when people have no interest in the conversation. Talking audibly on a phone thereby disrupts the attention of others. People are willing to relinquish privacy for their phone conversation for the convenience of talking wherever they happen to be. That convenience may be at the expense of other people's peace of mind. This violation of civility is an example of using public space as private space. As an indication of the emotional impact of incivility, Alkon presents herself—in the cover picture as well as in the text—as an avenging angel, rebuking individuals for lacking consideration. Her implicit message is that people are not only offended but desiring revenge when experiencing incivility. Incivility provokes strong negative emotions in others, potentially encouraging mistreatment in return. It is not clear how Alkon sees reciprocity and emotional contagion as bringing about change. These dynamics seem more likely to exaggerate the current situation.

Worklife is one of many life domains where people have concerns about incivility. The problem calls for a response from individuals, workgroups, and managers. Addressing the problem begins with clearly identifying the nature of incivility and of civility.

Definitions

A feature of intense academic focus on a topic is concept redundancy. When social scientists examine a phenomenon thoroughly, they notice variations. Some concepts separate into clear categories; others are subtle nuances. As Hershcovis (2011) explored in depth, the field of workplace mistreatment has generated a plethora of terms, "… including bullying (e.g., Rayner 1997), incivility (e.g., Andersson and Pearson 1999), social undermining (e.g., Duffy et al. 2002), mobbing (e.g., Leymann 1990), workplace aggression (e.g., Neuman and Baron 1998), emotional abuse (e.g., Keashly et al. 1997), victimization (e.g., Aquino et al. 1999), interpersonal conflict (e.g., Spector and Jex 1998), and abusive supervision (e.g., Tepper 2000)" (Hershcovis 2011, p. 499). She welcomed the close attention to the diverse forms of the phenomenon while cautioning against the field's fragmentation as researchers pursue one form of mistreatment without appreciating parallel work on other forms. Researchers tend to become aligned with and committed to a certain measure or language, reducing their openness to broader developments in the field. In a meta-analysis, she demonstrated that the constructs had little differential impact: for example, the predictive power of social undermining was not appreciably enhanced by additional measures of bullying or aggression. The bottom line was that mistreatment was the core issue; the specific form of mistreatment—whether it was bullying, social undermining, or incivility—was very much a secondary matter.

Hershcovis (2011) concluded by proposing a model that depicts workplace aggression as the generic phenomenon leading to a variety of distressing outcomes. The various forms of mistreatment arise through the operation of moderators (intent, intensity, frequency, etc.) of the relationship of workplace aggression with a variety of outcomes. The qualities that differentiate the various forms of workplace mistreatment include surface characteristics—frequency, intensity, and invisibility—of the offending behavior as well as qualities of the relationship between perpetrator and its target. Hershcovis (2011) questions how these differentiations make a meaningful contribution to understanding the processes to which they refer. It is worth considering that the commonalities across all forms of mistreatment are more salient than their differences.

Surface Characteristics

Hershcovis (2011) identifies three surface characteristics of mistreatment: frequency, intensity, and invisibility. Two of the surface characteristics are definitive in distinguishing among some of the widely used terms for mistreatment. Regarding frequency, definitions of bullying limit the term to situations that include multiple incidents over time (Hershcovis 2011). Regarding intensity, the most widely accepted definition limits incivility to low intensity behavior (Andersson and Pearson 1999). The third surface characteristic, invisibility, does not differentiate among the various forms of misbehavior, but serves to sustain misbehavior over time by avoiding reprimand against the perpetrator from those in authority (Baron et al. 1999). As workplace mistreatment becomes less acceptable to the point of being illegal in some jurisdictions, perpetrators become more adept at subtle forms of bad behavior.

The proposition that associates greater intensity of mistreatment with a stronger impact depicts incivility as parallel with physical aggression. Certainly, more intense physical assault results in more physical harm. A parallel process would propose that intense verbal abuse (screaming, cursing, etc.) generates greater distress than subtle incivility (rolling one's eyes, making a sarcastic remark). That is, the model proposes that the intensity of the mistreatment, regardless of its modality (physical aggression, sexual abuse, verbal abuse) produces harm in targets proportionally. The impact of intensity may be more complex.

The Risk Management Model proposes a nonlinear relationship of intensity with harm for non-contact forms of incivility (words, facial expressions, gestures, spatial positioning). First, language has a subtle complexity that far exceeds that of physical confrontation. People vary in their interpretation of a shrug but they are more likely to concur on the significance of a punch or a grope. Second, incivility has a trigger function regarding risk: any sign of disrespect flags problems with a working relationship. This quality is especially relevant in a time and place where blatant mistreatment of colleagues or subordinates prompts condemnation from the organization. Subtle cues would be the only ones available to people attempting to understand their status within the workplace community.

Specifically, the only form of mistreatment in Hershcovis's (2011) analysis that had a stronger relationship with an outcome than incivility was bullying that had a stronger correlation with physical wellbeing than did incivility. In contrast, incivility had stronger correlations with job satisfaction and turnover intention than did other forms of mistreatment. Abusive supervision did not have stronger correlations with outcomes than did incivility. One possible explanation for this finding could be the third surface characteristic: invisibility. Although the narrative that receives attention in popular media (This American Life 2010a, b) is the blatantly abusive boss, problematic supervisory relationships may be much more subtle. In displaying blatant abuse, bosses risk vulnerability to grievances from employees or reprimands from their superiors. They may also recognize that subtle shows of dominance gain more respect form bystanders than do blatant abuse.

Instead of a differential impact for intensity, the Risk Management Model proposes incivility as a threshold event. Regardless of whether incivility is blatant and intense or subtle and mild, incivility conveys increased risk. A line has been crossed. The strength of the association with distressing outcomes reflects qualities other than intensity. From this perspective, incivility need not be low intensity. The important definitional point is that incivility may have low intensity and still be a matter of consequence. Instead, frequency of incivility matters in that more frequent uncivil encounters suggest greater deterioration of the social environment of work with increased risk to its members.

Relationship Issues

The other qualities Hershcovis (2011) identified as moderators describe the relationship of perpetrators with targets: power differentials and intention. Power differentials give a quality to workplace mistreatment in that a party with greater power can inflict more harm on targets through physical strength, organizational authority, or influence. Research has reported that supervisor incivility has stronger relationships with job satisfaction, management trust, and turnover intentions than does coworker incivility, despite the greater frequency of coworker incivility (Leiter et al. 2011). The more consequential power of supervisors means that problems with the supervisory relationship present greater risks than do problems with collegial relationships. Supervisor incivility could have low intensity while communicating disrespect for the target employee. In contrast, incivility from fellow employees may have greater intensity or frequency but be viewed as less risky because of its more modest implications for career development. The stronger relationship of supervisor incivility with turnover intention supports this proposition from the Risk Management Model.

A second relationship quality is intent. The Andersson and Pearson (1999) definition of workplace incivility states that intention may be ambiguous. The definition encompasses the range of situations in which people find another person's behavior offensive or aggressive despite the supposed perpetrator lacking intent to harm. These situations may arise through thoughtlessness (an employee talks loudly in the hallway, disturbing the concentration of colleagues, despite bearing them no ill will) or a limited appreciation of the unintended impact of behavior (telling an off-color joke for the amusement of friends without appreciating that others may feel offended or even threatened by hearing the joke).

Regarding intent, research to date has established that targets' perception of intent is associated with greater impact of aggression (Aquino et al. 2001). However, the current state of research has not yet established that impact is associated with the actual intent from the perspective of the person generating the questionable behavior. Hershcovis (2011) rightly observed that more thorough-going paradigms that integrate the perspectives of diverse participants in social encounters are needed to address such questions.

It may be that intentional incivility conveys greater risk than incivility derived from thoughtlessness. Although the company of thoughtless colleagues may be unpleasant, it is not necessarily threatening. They may leave dirty dishes in the sink, fail to replace depleted coffee creamer, or use loud, obnoxious ringtones, but, aside from their serenity-destroying properties, these behaviors have little consequential impact. In contrast, intended incivility depicts perpetrators as making deliberate decisions to show disrespect or disdain towards targets. Simply, the perpetrators' expression of incivility suggests that they are confident that targets lack the power to reciprocate or to find protection. Whatever power differential was assumed prior to the uncivil act becomes exaggerated by the encounter if the target cannot promptly and convincingly respond. Intentional incivility could thereby present greater risk to targets than do unintended acts, regardless of the intensity of the incivility.

The Experience of Incivility

Models of workplace mistreatment often follow a linear model in which unpleasant treatment, arising for often unspecified reasons as exogenous factors, have an impact on victims leading to subsequent harm, such as career success or well-being (Cortina 2008; Hershcovis 2011; Pearson and Porath 2009). The more immediate perspective of the Risk Management model focuses on harm within the interaction itself.

An example of immediate harm comes from an interview with JoAnn Chiakulas, the only juror on the trial of former Illinois Governor Rod Blagojevich who believed he was innocent of trying to sell Barack Obama's senate seat (This American Life 2010a, b). She spoke of other jurors demeaning her as part of a strategy to change her vote. However, she was unable to give specific examples of demeaning statements. When pressed, she said that other jurors pointed out that "We have to convict him because the prosecution will have to retry the case if we don't." This statement is true (and Blagojevich was retired and subsequently found guilty of this charge) and not explicitly demeaning of Chiakulas. Another example was, "We'll be embarrassed if we don't find him guilty." This statement is not purely a statement of fact but it is not specifically demeaning of Chiakulas either. To some extent the lack of specific examples reflects the invisibility of incivility.

The demeaning quality is conveyed in the vocal inflections or expressions accompanying the words. To some extent, the impact of the exchange is the exchange itself. The subtle cues conveying incivility do not explicitly threaten future harm or retribution. The exchange in itself creates distress by excluding the target from the perpetrator's community. Isolation increases the target's vulnerability to risks within the group and when venturing outside of the group. Isolated people have a diminished capacity to address the hazards they encounter.

The Bright Side: The Role of Civility in Countering Risk

Civility encompasses a range of behaviors, words, and emotional tone that convey respect and acknowledge that the parties in the interaction share a community (Alderfer 1972; Herzberg et al. 1959). Civility is often associated with etiquette, suggesting that it follows rules of comportment that regulate behavior, keeping more base qualities of people in check (Elias 1982; Hartman 1996; Morris 1996). By managing one's behavior carefully within social discourse, people can demonstrate their membership in society, including the capacity to cross boundaries to interact with people of different social classes or occupations. In this way, civility has a quality of a common language that facilitates communication in a complex social world. This view of civility suggests that it may be insincere in that it masks one's true feelings behind a performance designed to convey an impression upon its audience (Lakoff 2006). While making discourse more manageable, this form of civility may also reduce its depth.

Civility has as well a less formal and more genuine quality when it conveys respect (Gilin-Oore et al. 2010). In contemporary work organizations, rules of comportment are less codified but showing respect remains critically important. In contrast to domains where bullying and abuse persist, many work environments across the industrialized world have an active, ongoing concern with respect. When working from a limited vision, the concern focuses more on avoiding unintended offence, as in political correctness, to prevent grievances charging implicit racism or sexism. In more value-driven settings, organizations have instituted interventions designed to increase civility as a means of showing respect and engaging employees more thoroughly in their work (Osatuke et al. 2009).

In its more genuine sense, civility in social interactions begins with being aware of the other person. At the most rudimentary level, simply perceiving the presence of another is an improvement over being unaware of sharing space with another person. Bumping into someone that whose presence went unnoticed seems rude. People may talk loudly or engage in other disruptive behaviors simply because they are not attending to the people around them. Going beyond simple awareness to acknowledging the other person conveys a greater degree of civility and respect. Although there are situations in which people prefer to be ignored, a nod, a greeting, or a conversation is generally well received because it conveys more respect and civility in most instances. Expressing appreciation and adapting one's behavior to accommodate others go even further in expressing respect. Both appreciation and accommodation convey awareness of the distinct qualities of the other person. These actions establish a more personal relationship with the other person by explicitly referring to the other person's distinct and positive qualities.

Research has established that civility among members of a workgroup is associated with more positive experiences of worklife. Leiter et al. (2011) in a sample of 1,107 hospital employees found team civility to be strongly correlated with respect ($r = .53$), efficacy ($r = .34$), job satisfaction ($r = .51$), commitment ($r = .43$), and management trust ($r = .39$). The relationship with management trust provides the most direct indicator of employees' assessment of risk. The civility assessed in this study referred to the interactions among colleagues and only incidentally referenced management. That is, greater civility among colleagues increased the extent to which employees felt that management was trustworthy.

The Leiter et al. (2011) study focused on improving civility within nursing units as discussed more thoroughly in Chap. 6. Bae et al. (2010, p. 41) have described nursing units as "the proximal context for individuals and a bounded interactive context created by nurses' attributes, interactions, and responses". The working relationships—with other nurses, supervisors, physicians, and patients—occurring within that context contribute to defining employees' identity. These relationships can provide individuals with access to extensive resources of expertise, practical assistance, or emotional support, increasing their confidence in their potential to thrive in their profession. When going badly, these relationships can generate intense emotional crises, increasing employees' sense of vulnerability. One response to increased riskiness is to seek transfers to other work units within the hospital or to leave the institution altogether to pursue their profession elsewhere (Shields and Ward 2001).

Core Propositions

Proposition 1: People want to Belong

The most basic proposition of the Risk Management model is that incivility frustrates the human motivation to belong. A sense of belonging is comforting. It conveys a sense of completeness and security. When that motive is unmet, people act to seek out relationships and group membership. When that motive is actively frustrated, people feel anxious with a sense of being at risk. From an evolutionary perspective, belonging to a group worked well for humans (Buss 1991). Individuals lacked the wherewithal to take on the beasts of the jungle, but as members of a coordinated group, they could defend themselves adequately. The people who survived and thrived were those who could maintain membership in a community. It has been proposed that loneliness served a survival function by motivating people towards group membership (Cacioppo et al. 2006). The immediate feeling of distress that occurs when experiencing loneliness prevents people from settling into an isolated lifestyle. Isolation was detrimental to both the lone individual as well as to the community that lacked sufficient membership to withstand the rigors of survival.

The advantages of belonging continue in a contemporary world with its increasingly complex social, economic, and cultural connections. Research has consistently found that participation in social groups improve individuals' sense of self-worth and confidence (Aquino and Thau 2009; Baumeister and Leary 1995). Group participation increases the capacity to trust and to build cooperative relationships (Stevens and Fiske 1975). Despite the scarcity of ferocious beasts, people continue to contend with a world that presents serious threats to their well-being. Career advancement and financial thriving require people to participate in large scale social institutions, such as businesses or government bureaucracies, as well as small scale groups, including project teams as well as ongoing workgroups. Not only is "being a team player" a nearly inevitable criterion for employment or promotion, opportunities for major accomplishments occur as part of a group. Advances in complex fields—computers, software, financial services, medicine, science—are created through a team effort. The lone genius is increasingly rare. The Nobel Prize goes to people who lead great teams effectively.

The survival function that belonging provided early in human evolution has continued throughout history to the present day. A social world, created by people, has become the overwhelmingly major aspect of the human environment. An active and fulfilling participation in a supportive workgroup remains a vital asset for people to thrive in that world. Incivility is not simply an unpleasant quality of a social interaction. Incivility communicates the perpetrators' understanding of their relationship to the target.

Proposition 2: People Notice

In light of the importance of belonging, it makes sense that people would have a refined capacity to interpret their standing with others. The capacities to both display emotion and to interpret the feelings of others accurately are skills that permit people to manage their participation in social groups. These capabilities have been recognized as fundamental to emotional intelligence (EI, Davies et al. 1998), and social competence (Eisenberg et al. 1998; Halberstadt et al. 2001). They constitute rudimentary social skills (Riggio 1986). They function as personal resources that people use to monitor their immediate social context.

Elfenbein et al. (2010) have demonstrated a strong relationship between these two skills: people who express well also perceive emotions accurately. The capacity to perceive feelings is also related to the extent to which people can convincingly display falsified emotions (Porter and ten Brinke 2008). Elfenbein and Ambady (2002) explored emotional eavesdropping: the capacity to accurately perceive emotions that the other person did not intend to convey. They operationalized the construct as the extent to which hearing a person's vocal inflections improved accuracy over simply seeing the other person's facial expression. This approach assumes that people exercise better control over their facial expressions than their vocal inflections that then becomes a leaky channel that could be read by those with sufficient perceptive ability.

From as early as 18 months, children show signs of having a capacity to figure out other people from observation. They are able to imitate others (Meltzoff 1995) and indicate that they can differentiate between intentional and accidental actions when imitating (Frith and Frith 2001; Leslie 1987). An observational study of preschool children found that five-year-olds used sophisticated strategies based upon reciprocity to elicit cooperation from their classmates (Leiter 1977). Frith and Frith (2001) argued that the speed and thoroughness with which children develop these capacities are evidence of a neurological foundation for a mentalizing system that represents links between people's intentions and their actions. This system underlies important qualities of emotional intelligence. Deficits in these neurological structures are candidates for explaining some of the social shortfalls displayed by children with autism (Mundy 2003). Overall, a large body of work has supported the proposition that humans have a structural disposition to scan their social environment, assigning intention and emotion to the people with whom they interact. These capacities are evident throughout human history and individual development.

Despite their sophisticated and diverse skills in social perception, people make mistakes. Applying simple heuristics to complex events contributes speed but creates errors. Two of the most common heuristics leading to errors are representative and availability (Maqsood et al. 2004; Tversky and Kahneman 1974). The representative heuristic applies familiar frameworks to new events. The availability heuristic arises from the relative ease of recalling large categories as opposed to small categories. Together, these cognitive patterns help to maintain the status quo. For example, a history of encountering incivility from a colleague may lead an employee to interpret a neutral or positive statement from that person as a criticism. These cognitive processes support the momentum arising from social dynamics, such as reciprocity, that perpetuate the current social climate of a work unit. That momentum resists change.

Research has produced consistent evidence of a long-standing human capacity for social perception. The sophistication of these capacities allows individuals to make the most of their opportunities within the complex networks of contemporary social environments. However, these abilities are not flawless. Cognitive limitations may contribute to the persistence of unpleasant social dynamics over time. Given the potential for impressions of other people to sustain over time, effective interventions require a way of challenging misperceptions.

The Risk Management Model proposes that a core function of social monitoring is risk assessment. The two-edged quality of social environments—as resources or threats—introduces considerable uncertainty. The anxiety prompted by uncertainty motivates people to seek information and to take action that

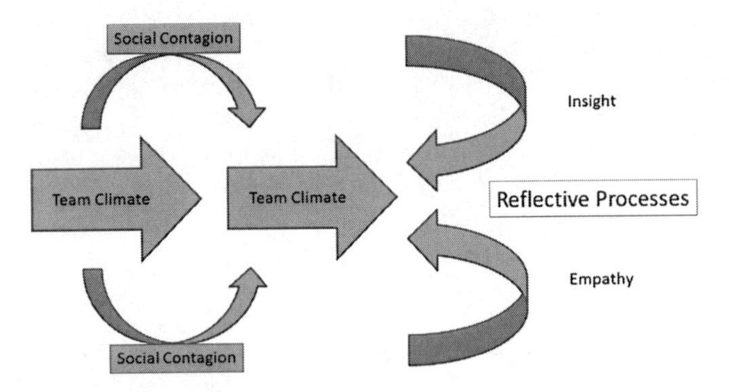

Fig. 2.1 Intervention as a reflective process

promises to reduce their exposure to risk. Often, the path of least resistance encourages people to fit into the existing social dynamic even if it is based upon unpleasant incivility and disrespect. Although people may be tempted to escape their current situation, they may encounter barriers to joining another group. A slow economic cycle may keep people constrained within unpleasant work-groups. In any case, people will seek ways to reduce their exposure to the risks signaled by workplace incivility (Fig. 2.1).

Conclusion

Incivility and civility are modes of behavior that reflect the extent to which people anticipate, accommodate, and explicitly appreciate other people. In some contexts, people judge civility by the thoroughness with which people follow rules of etiquette. In other situations—and perhaps most contemporary situations—the critical issue is showing consideration for others without explicit reference to a code of conduct. Consideration presents challenges in that it requires people to consider another person's perspective. Consideration shares this quality with empathy. A modest level of consideration in line with pseudo-empathy asks, "Would I be bothered by someone conducting a loud phone conversation nearby?" A more sophisticated level of consideration makes an effort to acknowledge that others may differ in what they would experience as irritating.

In contrast to civility that characterizes the overall level of demeanor or climate in a workgroup, incivility exists as discrete events. When people report experiencing incivility, aggression, or psychological abuse at work, they rarely mean a constant barrage of these events. Specific forms of incivility occurred a few times a year or less (Leiter et al. 2011). As noted by the Risk Management Model, incivility represents a threshold event: an incident does not open the door to constant harassment, but it signals a more risky social environment.

These definitional issues raise questions as to the source of workplace incivility and its consequences. Related to these questions is understanding what sustains incivility among people who work together. Given the unpleasant nature of incivility and the dangers inherent in an uncivil social environment, is seems that an active process is necessary to sustain a dysfunctional environment over time.

References

Advisory Board Company. (2009). *Managing disruptive behaviors: Creating a healthy workplace culture*. DC: Washington.

Alderfer, C. P. (1972). *Existence, relatedness, and growth; Human needs in organizational setting*. New York: Free Press.

Alkon, A. (2010). *I see rude people*. New York: McGraw-Hill.

Andersson, L. M., & Pearson, C. M. (1999). Tit for tat? The spiraling effect of incivility in the workplace. *The Academy of Management Review, 24*, 452–471.

Aquino, K., Grover, S. L., Bradfield, M., & Allen, D. G. (1999). The effects of negative affectivity, hierarchical status, and self-determination on workplace victimization. *Academy of Management Journal, 42*, 260–272.

Aquino, K., & Thau, S. (2009). Workplace victimization: Aggression from the target's perspective. *Annual Review of Psychology, 60*, 717–741.

Aquino, K., Tripp, T. M., & Bies, R. J. (2001). How employees respond to personal offense: The effects of blame attribution, victim status, and offender status on revenge and reconciliation in the workplace. *Journal of Applied Psychology, 86*, 52–59.

Bae, S. H., Mark, B., & Fried, B. (2010). Impact of nursing unit turnover on patient outcomes in hospitals. *Journal of Nursing Scholarship, 42*, 40–49.

Baron, R. A., Neuman, J. H., & Geddes, D. (1999). Social and personal determinants of workplace aggression: Evidence for the impact of perceived injustice and the type A behavior pattern. *Aggressive Behavior, 25*, 281–296.

Baumeister, R. F., & Leary, M. R. (1995). The need to belong: Desire for interpersonal attachments as a fundamental human motivation. *Psychological Bulletin, 117*, 497–529.

Buss, D. M. (1991). Evolutionary personality psychology. *Annual Review of Psychology, 42*, 459–491.

Cacioppo, J. T., Hughes, M. E., Waite, L. J., Hawkley, L. C., & Thisted, R. A. (2006). Loneliness as a specific risk factor for depressive symptoms: Cross-sectional and longitudinal analyses. *Psychology and Aging, 21*, 140–151.

Cortina, L. M. (2008). Unseen injustice: Incivility as modern discrimination in organizations. *Academy of Management Review, 33*, 55–57.

Davies, M., Stankov, L., & Roberts, R. D. (1998). Emotional intelligence: In search of an elusive construct. *Journal of Personality and Social Psychology, 75*, 989–1015.

Duffy, M. K., Ganster, D. C., & Pagon, M. (2002). Social undermining in the workplace. *Academy of Management Journal, 45*, 331–351.

Eisenberg, N., Cumberland, A., & Spinrad, T. L. (1998). Parental socialization of emotion. *Psychology Inquiry, 9*, 241–273.

Elfenbein, H. A., & Ambady, N. (2002). Predicting workplace outcomes from the ability to eavesdrop on feelings. *Journal of Applied Psychology, 87*, 963–971.

Elfenbein, H. A., Foo, M. D., Mandal, M., Biswal, R., Eisenkraft, N., Lim, A., et al. (2010). Individual differences in the accuracy of expressing and perceiving nonverbal cues: New data on an old question. *Journal of Research in Personality, 44*, 199–206.

Elias, N. (1982). *The history of manners*. New York: Pantheon.

Frith, U., & Frith, C. (2001). The biological basis of social interaction. *Current Directions in Psychologic Science, 10*, 151–155.

Gilin-Oore, D., LeBlanc, D., Day, A., Leiter, M. P., Laschinger, H. K. S., Price, S. L., Latimer, M. (2010). When respect deteriorates: Incivility as a moderator of the stressor-strain relationship among hospital workers. *Journal of Nursing Management, 18*, 878–888.

Halberstadt, A. G., Denham, S. A., & Dunsmore, J. C. (2001). Affective social competence. *Social Development, 10*, 79–119.

Hartman, E. (1996). *Organizational ethics*. Oxford: Oxford University Press.

Hershcovis, M. S. (2011). Incivility, social undermining, bullying… oh my!: A call to reconcile constructs within workplace aggression research. *Journal of Organizational Behavior, 32*, 499–519.

Herzberg, F., Mausner, B., & Snyderman, B. B. (1959). *The motivation to work*. New York: John Wiley.

Hutchinson, M., Vickers, M., Jackson, D., & Wilkes, L. (2005). I'm gonna do what I wanna do: Organizational change as a legitimized vehicle for bullies. *Health Care Manager, 30*, 331–336.

Keashly, L. (1998). Emotional abuse in the workplace: Conceptual and empirical issues. *Journal of Emotional Abuse, 1*, 85–117.

Keashly, L., & Jagatic, K. (2000, January). *Workplace abuse and aggression*. Paper presented at Workplace Bullying 2000: Redefining Harassment, Oakland, CA.

Keashly, L., Hunter, S., & Harvey, S. (1997). Abusive interaction and role state stressors: Relative impact on student residence assistant stress and work attitudes. *Work & Stress, 11*, 175–185.

Lakoff, R. (2006). Civility and its discontents: Or, getting in your face. In R Lakoff, & S. Ide (Eds.), *Broadening the horizon of linguistic politeness* (pp.23–43). Amsterdam/Philadelphia: John Benjamins.

Leiter, M. P. (1977). A study of reciprocity in preschool play groups. *Child Development, 48*, 1288–1295.

Leiter, M. P., Laschinger, H. K. S., Day, A., & Gilin-Oore, D. (2011). The impact of civility interventions on employee social behavior, distress, and attitudes. *Journal of Applied Psychology, 96*, 1258–1274.

Leiter, M. P., Price, S. L., & Laschinger, H. K. S. (2010). Generational differences in distress, Attitudes and incivility among nurses. *Journal of Nursing Management, 18*, 970–980.

Leslie, A. M. (1987). Pretense and representation: The origins of theory of mind. *Psychological Review*, 94, 412–426.

Leymann, H. (1990). Mobbing and psychological terror at workplaces. *Violence and Victims, 5*, 119–126.

Maqsood, T., Finegan, A. D., & Walker, D. H. T. (2004). Biases and heuristics in judgment and decision making: The dark side of tacit knowledge. *Issues in Informing Science and Information Technology, 1*, 295–301. Retrieved January 6, 2012, from http://articles.iisit.org/050maqso.pdf.

Meltzoff, Am. N. (1995). Understanding the interactions of others: Re-enactment of intended acts by 18-month-old children. *Developmental Psychology, 31*, 838–850.

Mills, S. (2012). Impoliteness in a cultural context. *Journal of Pragmatics*, online. http://teaching.shu.ac.uk.

Morand, D. A. (2003). Politeness and the clash of interaction orders in cross-cultural communication. *Thunderbird International Business Review, 45*, 521–540.

Morris, J. (1996). *Democracy beguiled* (pp. 24–35). Autumn: The Wilson Quarterly.

Mundy, P. (2003). The neural basis of social impairments in autism: the role of the dorsal medial-frontal cortex and anterior cingulate system. *Journal of Child Psychology and Psychiatry, 44*, 793–809.

Namie, G., & Namie, R. (2000). *The bully at work: What you can do to stop the hurt and reclaim your dignity on the job*. Naperville: Sourcebooks, Inc.

Namie, G. (2007). The challenge of workplace bullying. *Employee Relations Today, 34*(2), 43–51.

Neuman, J. H., & Baron, R. A. (1998). Workplace violence and workplace aggression: Evidence concerning specific forms, potential causes, and preferred targets. *Journal of Management, 24*, 391–419.

Niedhammer, I., David, S., Degioanni, S., et al. (2000). Workplace bullying and sleep disturbances: findings from a large scale cross-sectional survey in the French working population. *Sleep, 32*, 1211–1219.

Osatuke, K., Mohr, D., Ward, C., Moore, S. C., Dyrenforth, S., & Belton, L. (2009). Civility, respect, engagement in the workforce (CREW): Nationwide organization development intervention at Veterans Health Administration. *Journal of Applied Behavioral Science, 45*, 384–410.

Pearson, C., & Porath, C. (2009). *The Cost of Bad Behavior: how incivility is damaging your business and what to do about it*. New York: Penguin.

Porter, S., & ten Brinke, L. (2008). Reading between the lies: Identifying concealed and falsified emotions in universal facial expressions. *Psychological Science, 19*, 508–514.

Rayner, C. (1997). The incidence of workplace bullying. *Journal of Community & Applied Social Psychology, 7*, 199–208.

Riggio, R. E. (1986). Assessment of basic social skills. *Journal of Personality and Social Psychology, 51*, 649–660.

Schat, A. C. H., Frone, M. R., & Kelloway, E. K. (2006). Prevalence of workplace aggression in the US workforce: Findings from a national study. In E. K. Kelloway, J. Barling, & J. J. Hurrell Jr. (Eds.), *Handbook of workplace violence* (pp. 47–90). Thousand Oaks: Sage.

Shields, M. A., & Ward, M. (2001). Improving nurse retention in the National Health Service in England: The impact of job satisfaction on intention to quit. *Journal of Health Economics, 20*, 677–701.

Spector, P. E., & Jex, S. M. (1998). Development of four self-report measures of job stressors and strain: Interpersonal conflict at work scale, organizational constraints scale, quantitative workload inventory, and physical symptoms inventory. *Journal of Occupational Health Psychology, 3*, 356–367.

Taylor, S. E., & Fiske, S. T. (1975). Point of view and perceptions of causality. *Journal of Personality and Social Psychology, 32*, 439–445.

Tepper, B. J. (2000). Consequences of abusive supervision. *Academy of Management Journal, 43*, 178–190.

This American Life (2010a). *Last man standing*. Retrieved February 14, 2012, from http://www.thisamericanlife.org/radio-archives/episode/421/last-man-standing.

This American Life (2010b). *Petty tyrant*. Retrieved February 14, 2012, from http://www.thisamericanlife.org/radio-archives/episode/419/transcript.

Truss, L. (2005). *Talk to the hand: The utter bloody rudeness of everyday life (or six good reasons to stay home and bolt the door*. London: Profile.

Tversky, A., & Kahneman, D. (1974). Judgment under uncertainty: Heuristics and biases. *Science, 185*, 1124–1131.

Yamada, D. (2000). The phenomenon of workplace bullying and the need for status-blind hostile work environment protection'. *Georgetown Law Journal, 88*, 475–536.

Zapf, D., Einarsen, S., Hoel, H., & Vartia, M. (2003). Empirical findings on bullying in the workplace. In S. Einarsen, H. Hoel, D. Zapf, & C. Cooper (Eds.), *Bullying and emotional abuse in the workplace: International perspectives in research and practice* (pp. 102–126). London: Taylor & Francis.

Chapter 3
Causes and Consequences of Workplace Mistreatment

Abstract This chapter considers the social context of incivility as a major force in perpetuating the quality of behavior within a worksetting. Both organizational policies and management practices influence the social climate of a workgroup. Leadership plays a critical role both in the symbolic value of leaders' interactions with people within the organization as well as their actions in response to violations of civility norms. The extent to which civility or incivility dominates a workgroup's culture has consequences for the wellbeing of employees and the organization's productivity. The chapter concludes with a reflection on the multiple directions of causal influence in social networks.

Causes and Consequences of Workplace Incivility

A persistent question about workplace incivility is its persistence. Given the importance to individuals of a sense of community and belonging, it would seem that group cultures would be self-correcting. It seems reasonable to expect cultures to have processes that put their dynamics back on track whenever they experience discord. It may well be that such processes operate most of the time: most workplaces operate smoothly. In our surveys, half of respondents report that they have experienced no incivility from colleagues in the past year (Leiter et al. 2011). However, it is also clear that self-correcting processes do not operate effectively all of the time. An important part of a model is developing an explanation for the occurrence of incivility and especially its persistence in problematic workgroups.

M. Leiter, *Analyzing and Theorizing the Dynamics of the Workplace Incivility Crisis*, SpringerBriefs in Psychology,
DOI: 10.1007/978-94-007-5571-0_3,

Proposition 3: Workgroup Climates are Self-Perpetuating

Workplace incivility would be a much smaller problem if it only occurred in response to unusual circumstances, such as the perpetrator having a stressful time on the morning commute. The problem represents a much larger problem to the extent that incivility reflects a breakdown of values within a workplace community. It goes beyond an individual problem to be a workgroup breakdown. The Risk Management Model views each workplace as having a somewhat unique culture that arises from the interplay of values as they are reflected in the day-to-day interactions among members of that workgroup. Addressing workplace civility requires a direct consideration of social dynamics.

Mills (2009) cautioned against viewing culture as a set of rules to judge individual behavior. Instead, she recommends the notion of community of practice that constitutes the enacted behaviors and words that a community has instituted in its day-to-day interactions (Wenger 1998). Workplaces have the appropriate scale for a community of practice in that they bring together a group of people who interact with one another in the course of fulfilling their responsibilities. The nature of their interactions is informed both by the larger culture as well as by the norms of their occupation. Distinct patterns of conversation and behavior convey respect while others are dismissive or even offensive. The primary question is identifying participants' reactions to one another's behavior rather than judging how carefully individuals follow pre-ordained rules of etiquette.

Predictors of Ongoing Workplace Incivility

The civility level of a worksetting does not arise accidently. It reflects the workgroup's larger socioeconomic context, the backgrounds of its members, cognitive operations (heuristics and rationales), the values of workgroup leaders, and the larger organizational policies governing the workgroup. The previous chapter reflected on the larger socioeconomic/cultural context of incivility. These qualities provide a backdrop for workgroup communities. Within that broad context, some workgroups develop supportive, creative communities while others have social environments that are dull and uninspiring. Of particular interest in this chapter are the qualities that lead some workgroups to become uncivil or even toxic social settings.

Overall, workgroup civility reflects a variety of influences. No one group or individual has sole responsibility for a group's civility. This condition absolves anyone from being individually accountable for relationship problems, but also means that no one factor can single-handedly improve workgroup civility. Shared problems call for shared solutions.

The following sections consider three domains that have implications for workplace civility: management factors, organizational policies, and individual characteristics. These domains encompass qualities of leadership as well as organizational systems as relevant and influential. However, everything does not happen at the system level: individuals play an important role as well. A complete picture of workgroup culture requires multiple perspectives.

Management Factors

In their broad overview of research on workplace mistreatment, Aquino and Thau (2009) found that the most powerful predictors of workplace mistreatment were higher level management failures. An important element is the behavior of leaders themselves: authoritarian leadership styles modeled disregard for the quality of relationships among people within the organization.

First, abrupt communications and demonstrated disregard for subordinates' perspectives on issues important to their worklife convey disrespect from leaders. In turn, employees copy this tone in their exchanges with one another. Communicating in an authoritarian manner conveys the assumption that a position of authority has an exalted status deserving of greater respect than the subordinate. For parties who fully accept the authority structure, the tone and manner of authoritarian communication seems appropriate. For observers or participants who assume an egalitarian perspective, authoritarian communications express incivility towards the subordinate in that it devalues the subordinates' status as a person (Leiter and Stright 2009). The quality of these interactions set the tone for the organizational culture. Specifically, one way to emulate those in authority is to communicate with colleagues in disrespectful ways to imply that one has greater status (Isaac 2011; Skogstad et al. 2007). Behaving in an authoritarian, disrespectful fashion could be part of a strategy for advancement in the organization but only in a culture that tolerates or extols disrespect.

Second, authoritarian leadership also contributes to workplace mistreatment by drawing sharper boundaries between groups of employees. Clear differentiation among groups of employees increases the risk of incivility across boundaries. People apply different standards to their behavior towards out-group members than towards in-group members. Cortina (2008) proposed that much of workplace incivility derives from deep-seated racism and sexism. With stronger organizational and cultural sanctions for explicit expressions of racial and sexual prejudice, people give voice to these views through rude behavior towards one another. She provides a detailed example of women attorneys receiving less respectful behavior than their male colleagues in the USA federal court system. Cortina's argument concerns differential behavior arising from discrimination based on identifiable personal characteristics that may pertain as well to discrimination based upon professional boundaries (e. g., physicians vs. nurses), hierarchy (bosses vs. subordinates), or occupational group (medical record clerks vs. accounting clerks) (Crocker and Major 1989; Crocker et al. 1991). Differences in in-group and out-group membership is associated with distinct attribution patterns for experiences of mistreatment (Hershcovis and Barling 2010). A dominant theme across these theories and conceptual models is that social systems that separate people into distinct categories face a challenge in maintaining civil exchanges across the boundaries of those categories. Leadership behaviors and communications influence the rigidity of those boundaries. Senior leaders may decry bureaucratic silos within their companies but allocate resources and authority along departmental lines in ways that reinforce their separation.

Addressing workplace mistreatment requires an executive level commitment to demonstrate active endorsement of valuing workplace civility (Davenport et al. 1999). Without active effort promoting civility, the level of respect expressed among people can deteriorate.

The second major contributor to mistreatment identified by Aquino and Thau (2009) was insufficient direction regarding appropriate collegial behavior. Lack of direction and overall role ambiguity was associated with greater victimization (Agervold and Mikkelsen 2004) when senior leaders leave it to employees to establish their style of communication. This approach to leadership aggravates risks inherent in the existing organizational culture, the personal civility of its incoming employees, and impact of organizational change. First, an existing culture, as noted earlier, has momentum. Without active structuring or exogenous influences, the existing culture will perpetuate itself over time. As indicated by the high level of autocorrelation in many measures of employees' work experiences (cf. Maslach and Leiter 2008), the psychological connections people make with their workplaces have stability over years. Workplaces lacking a climate of civility and respect are unlikely to develop those qualities without external pressures. Evidence of incivility spirals have identified situations in which incivility accelerates into more aggressive forms of mistreatment (Pearson et al. 2005). In contrast to a steady state dynamic, an internal development process or an external force tips the balance in the wrong direction towards greater incivility.

Relying on the personal civility of incoming personnel to shape the future of a workgroup culture creates risks from the level civility as well as the diversity of personal histories those new employees bring with them. In an increasingly diverse workforce in the post-industrialized world, it is reasonable to expect that incoming employees would have different standards and criteria for evaluating one another's civility. Cultures not only differ in strictness in observing etiquette as expressions of respect, they also differ in the behaviors that convey these qualities. In some cultures, voicing disagreement signals disrespect for authority; in other cultures it signals an avid interest in and commitment to the topic of discussion. As noted in the introduction, many see a crisis in civility throughout the life domains. With questionable levels of civility in society organizations cannot reasonably expect new employees to arrive with an inherent sense of conveying civility and respect among colleagues. Professional education has been identified as a source of stereotypes towards members of other professions (Wilson and Pirrie 2000). For example, doctors may have different views of what constitutes civility towards nurses than nurses would view as appropriate behavior (Carpenter 1995; MacKay 1992). It has been recommended that active promotion of effective, sensitive communication is an essential part of preparing health care providers for inter-professional collaboration (Choi and Pak 2006). Without active training and encouragement, employees are unlikely to change appreciatively from their distinct professional perspective.

Organizational change carries the risk of prompting a negative spiral. Although change would be welcomed for a unit that has settled into a dysfunctional pattern of incivility, change for the better may be exceptional. A dysfunctional group would be likely to resist change actively. Incivility among coworkers is associated with lower trust of management (Gilin-Oore et al. 2010). Whereas many changes in contemporary health care follow the model of 'doing more with less,' employees often confront diminishing resources along with constant if not growing demand. These conditions have the potential to increase conflict among team members.

Together, these influences reduce the potential for problematic worksettings to improve on their own. The inter-connected network of relationships among employees serves to maintain the status quo in most circumstances. When internal or external influences prompt a problematic workgroup to change, their sense of mistrust of management and of one another will resist change. Should resistance fail, the group faces a threat of worsening rather than improving.

Organizational Policies and Legislation

The thoroughness with which organizations develop, implement, and apply policies to address workplace mistreatment provides a means through which senior management influences the social environment of workgroups. Research has determined that inadequate or laxly enforced policies are a major contributor to chronic mistreatment (O'Moore and Lynch 2007). Because of reluctance by first line managers and colleagues to access existing policies, active training programs can contribute to the policies' success (Daniel 2006). Employees often view these policies with skepticism. They will monitor their implementation to determine whether they actually resolve problems situations or perpetuate them (Harvey et al. 2006). Policy implementation must address a concern—borne out by employee observation and experience—that victims of mistreatment often feel further victimized after they made complaints (Daniel 2006). In some settings, management has a history of blaming the victims or resenting the demands on leadership inherent in complaints from targets of mistreatment. These considerations suggest that articulating a policy is only one step towards addressing workplace mistreatment.

The details of policy implementation require the coordinated action of multiple parties. Cowen (2011) reported that human resource professionals identify gaps between their organization's policies and the problems that they were developed to address. For example, an issue with workplace bullying laws is that they are developed to go beyond previous legal standards designed to address discrimination against visible minorities. In contrast, anti-bullying legislation strives to provide legal recourse to employees who are not members of visible minorities but who nonetheless believe they are subject to mistreatment on the basis of personal dislike or simply inappropriate behavior from perpetrators (Lopez et al. 2009).

Canada and European nations have enacted anti-bullying laws without reference to membership in protected groups, working from a premise that employees have a right to being treated with respect at work. The United States does not have a tradition of developing laws to control harassment on the idea of individual dignity (Harthill 2008). Stone (2009) raises a variety of concerns about anti-bullying legislation that apply as well to organizational policies. She argues that the assumptions and frameworks underlying anti-discrimination policies do not seamlessly translate to informing anti-bullying policies.

The Risk Management Model proposes that mistreatment poses a threat to identity. This threat not only prompts a cautious approach to workplace interactions, it also follows people will engage in remedial identity work in the wake of encountering mistreatment (Lutgen-Sandvik 2008). Men and women in aggregate differ in their preferred mode of remedial identity work (Ashcraft 2000; Ashforth and Humphrey 1993); their propensity to access formal procedures to address mistreatment may be a difference with a consequential impact.

One problem Stone (2009) identifies for legal remedies to workplace bullying is the wide range of behaviors that fall within its definition. As noted at the beginning of Chap. 2, definitions are inconsistent on core issues of frequency, the types of behavior included, intentionality, and the relative status of those involved. A given perpetrator may vary behavior over time, including name calling, sarcasm, threats to job security, insults, stealing credit, screaming, and other actions. It is difficult to identify specific behaviors as clearly abusive. Legislators prefer to have these points pinned down but the dynamics of workplace mistreatment do not readily fit into legal definitions.

A central question reflected in the evolution of legal sanctions for workplace mistreatment is the extent to which the law leads or follows social change. One enduring perspective is that law reflects social values and must remain close to the prevailing norms; the contrasting view is that legislation can shape society by stipulating norms that better reflect an ideal society.

These considerations suggest serious limitations to a proscriptive approach to controlling workplace incivility. Specific behaviors that signal incivility overlap with behaviors that convey humor or even active support for colleagues. Legal sanctions can serve a constructive role in responding to egregious violations of workplace behavioral norms, but they have a limited impact on actively developing a vibrant workplace culture.

Individual Characteristics

Individuals play an active role in the occurrence of workplace mistreatment. They are not simply cogs in the wheels spun by organizational or management factors. When surveying workplaces, the data shows distinct patterns at the level of both workgroups and of the individuals within those groups. People bring enduring personality characteristics to the workplace as well as habitual ways of perceiving situations or responding to demands. It would be unreasonable to expect everyone within a workgroup to react identically to events.

Not surprisingly, perpetrators of mistreatment at work were found to show greater evidence of aggressive personality traits than do their colleagues (Matthiesen and Einarsen 2007). Targets of workplace mistreatment scored lower on self-esteem in this survey of Norwegian employees. Other surveys of Norwegian employees found that perpetrators of workplace mistreatment report having interpersonal problems at work, but not at a level that clearly differentiates them from their colleagues (Glasø et al. 2009). Interpersonal problems at work appear to be a widespread issue to which people have a wide range of reactions. This study also found that supervisors whom employees perceive as being abusive often are unaware of their impact on others and are unaware of any intent to harm others. When considering small businesses, Kets de Vries (1985) noted that entrepreneurs often have a history of interpersonal problems at work. Escaping problematic environments contributes to their motivation to start their own businesses. Meglich and Eesley (2011) proposed that many entrepreneurs have weak management skills, leaving them to revert more readily to poor and even unethical supervisory behavior. The personal investment they have made in the business may aggravate anxiety, especially when the business goes badly.

Douglas and Martinko (2001) found a cluster of personality characteristics associated with instigating workplace mistreatment. The cluster included trait anger, favorable attitudes about revenge, and a tendency to attribute negative workplace experiences to other people. The cluster was especially closely related to instigating mistreatment for people with a low level of self-control.

Leiter et al. (2010, August) explored rudeness rationales as attributions through which people justify uncivil behavior towards others. They identified three rationales used in their sample of Canadian health care providers: pressure, toughness, and sensitivity. The pressure rational justifies incivility as an uncharacteristic slip due to stressful demands. The instigator apologizes for losing control in tight circumstances. The toughness rationale justifies incivility as an unpleasant but necessary part of the instigator's role. Because colleagues lack initiative, the instigator must talk tough to prompt them into action at work. With the sensitivity rationale the instigator denies that the behavior was uncivil. The problem is that the target lacks the fortitude or sense of humor to realize that the behavior was not only appropriate but desirable. To varying degrees, the rationales absolve the perpetrator of responsibility for the impact of uncivil behavior.

Rudeness rationales are largely an individual proclivity, but they have a workgroup level dimension as well. Within a group's culture, each rationale may be supported or actively rejected. To the extent to which instigators feel justified in behaving uncivilly, they are likely to behave that way in the future.

Conclusion

Management factors play a critical role in the development and persistence of incivility within a workplace culture. Policies have a beneficial impact only to the extent that they are competently managed. Individual limitations in civility are most evident when managers behave badly towards their employees. The capacity of managers to monitor their workgroup, respond to incidents of mistreatment, implement effective policies, and model respectful behavior contributes to the quality of a workgroup culture. In addition to personal contact with managers, employees are influenced by the organization's policies and procedures. In addition to conveying the core values of the organization, policies shape the day-to-day priorities for employees, including the extent to which civility really matters. Finally, individual personality qualities and attribution processes play a role. Employees do not simply respond to their environmental conditions but contribute to defining them.

Consequences

Workplace incivility has been associated with negative outcomes for individual employees and for the organizations that employ them. Individuals experience the distress from incivility as stress, anxiety, and depression (Yamada 2000). Organizations experience a reduction in productivity (Bies and Tripp 1996) that can evolve at times into retaliation directed towards the organization (Skarlicki and Folger 1997).

Personal distress arising from workplace mistreatment covers a full range of indicators. Research has identified relationships with decreased mental health as indicted by depression and anxiety (Hansen et al. 2006; Tepper 2000) and emotional exhaustion (Grandey et al. 2007). Somatic symptoms of job stress, such as gastro-intestinal disturbance and headaches may accompany psychiatric symptoms (LeBlanc and Kelloway 2002). More specific to the workplace are consistent associations of mistreatment with job burnout (Cortina et al. 2001; Keashly et al. 1997; Leiter et al. 2011).

Regarding workplace behavior, mistreatment is associated with overall withdrawal from work as indicated by absences (Hauge et al. 2010; Kivimaki et al. 2000), diminished engagement, and increased turnover (Baba et al. 1999; Cortina et al. 2001; Chiaburu and Harrison 2008; Leiter and Maslach 2009). In general, workplace incivility creates uncertainty that is distressing to endure. Without a clear path to resolving that uncertainty, people will seek to escape from that setting, hoping to find a safer work environment.

On a general level, the experience of receiving incivility prompts feelings of ostracism and injustice leading to psychological distress combined with a desire to disengage from the worksetting (Caza and Cortina 2007). The impact appears to stretch beyond the worksetting with greater work/family conflict (Lim and Lee 2011). Pearson and Porath (2009) laid out the most thorough list of consequences in their approach to calculating the financial impact of incivility, showing evidence that a company with a billion dollars of revenue attributed 71 million in costs annually to workplace incivility in the USA.

A growing body of evidence demonstrates that incivility is costly in terms of personal distress, organizational performance, and revenue. The research field faces serious challenges in precisely calculating these costs in the workplace in that mistreatment eludes definition by taking so many forms, its existence depends somewhat on recipients' interpretation, and reporting of incivility is not thorough. Converging evidence supports the contention that incivility incurs a broad range of costs, some of which are serious and enduring.

Overall, employees experience workplace incivility as illegitimate demands (Semmer and Schallberger 1996) that undermine the psychological safety of their workplace (Edmondson 1999). Illegitimate demands, in addition to legitimate work demands, overwhelm employees' coping resources. Further aggravating that demand/resource imbalance is the loss of resources arising from low levels of civility: uncivil relationships do not simply occupy time that could otherwise be devoted to civil relationships, they have a potential of undermining the social environment more extensively. First, through an incivility spiral (Pearson et al. 2005) other colleagues may follow an uncivil code of conduct. Second, as employees perceive greater riskiness in the work environment, they hesitate to engage in supportive interactions with colleagues. These dynamics may result in perpetuating the consequences of incivility well past the actual incidents.

The Positive View: Civility has Impact

Social perception, along with other aspects of emotional intelligence, has been proposed to be a fundamental part of leadership skills, allowing the development of stronger connections to others and inspiring confidence in the group's prospects (Walter and Bruch 2008). In short, social perception is a valuable resource for getting along in the world. It not only helps people to participate in their social world, it functions as an effective tool for advancing to leadership roles. Civility among colleagues is associated with reduced burnout. Civil interactions identify colleagues as potential resources upon whom employees can call to help manage work demands, maintaining a viable balance of resources with demands. Civility is associated with greater professional efficacy (Halbesleben 2006; Leiter and Maslach 1988) that can buffer employees from reacting to workplace demands with burnout (Liang and Hsieh 2008). Instead of the exhausting, distancing, and discouraging impact of incivility, civil collegial relationships have the potential to be energizing, involving, and empowering.

In addition to generating a sense of wellbeing, civility is associated with more positive attitudes at work. Civility has been linked to increased organizational commitment and job satisfaction (Chiaburu and Harrison 2008; Cortina et al. 2001; Trudel 2010). Consistent with propositions of the Risk Management Model, increased management trust is associated not only with supervisor civility but with coworker civility as well (Cook and Wall 1980; Laschinger and Finegan 2005). In parallel, increased civility is associated with more positive views on justice in workplace decisions (Kramer 1999) partially due to improved interactional justice in the decision making process (Berkowitz 1993; Bies 2000; Bies and Moag 1986). It is not simply that incivility prompts job dissatisfaction as reported by Cortina et al. (2001). From a positive psychology perspective, civility is an active force contributing to the quality of a workplace environment.

Nomological Network of Civility

Considering the antecedents and consequences of civility or incivility encourages a linear view of causality. An event or existing condition (cause) influences an individual's experience (mediator) that encourages either civility or incivility (consequence). This sequence makes sense. Another sequence that also makes sense is that one person's uncivil action (cause) prompts an emotional reaction (mediation) from a colleague who seeks to withdraw from the worksetting (consequence). Both sequences make sense and provide ways to generate testable hypotheses about the sources and impact of social behavior at work. However, they have a limited capacity to capture the complex dynamics of workplace communities.

An alternative approach is to consider workplace communities as nomological networks lacking clearly defined starting points and endpoints. This perspective is useful when considering the overall pattern of correlations among a group of constructs (cf. Ackerman et al. 2005; Spreitzer 1995). When an observer—a casual observer or a systematic researcher—enters a worksetting, it has already established an equilibrium in social dynamics among the individuals and groups that define that community. A cross-sectional survey that assesses employees' views of management, their level of work engagement, indicators of distress, and various dimensions of their ongoing social contact with their colleagues and supervisors will provide a snapshot reflecting the overall balance of these qualities with one another. To analyze these relationships with multiple regression, it is necessary to designate one indicator, such as cynicism, as an outcome of other variables. However, it also makes sense that an employees' level of cynicism could influence the social behavior they initiate and the reactions they received from colleagues. This pattern is at times labeled 'reversed causality' (Sonnentag et al. 2010) that is somewhat misleading in that it implies that one direction of influence is secondary to another. Few research studies implement the interventions procedures with thorough experimental controls that are necessary to establish directional causality conclusively. The level of evidence that is more readily available in cross-sectional and longitudinal surveys are more convincingly viewed as providing information on the nomological network among the elements.

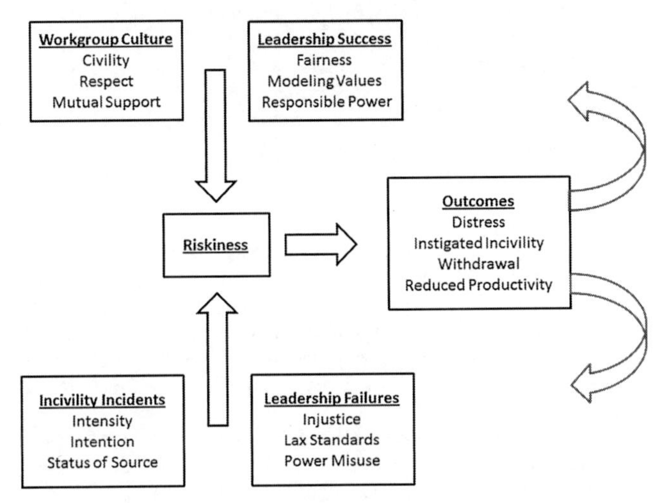

The diagram summarizes the major points in the model. Riskiness lies at the center. A positive workgroup culture supplemented and supported by constructive leadership behavior reduces risk. In the contrary direction, incivility in conjunction with leadership failures increases riskiness. Greater riskiness results in personal distress, more instigated incivility, withdrawal, and reduced productivity for the unit. These outcomes in turn participate in spirals that tend to perpetuate the current situation.

References

Ackerman, P. L., Beier, M. E., & Boyle, M. O. (2005). Working memory and intelligence: The same or different constructs? *Psychological Bulletin, 131*, 30–60.

Agervold, M., & Mikkelsen, E. G. (2004). Relationships between bullying, psychosocial work environment and individual stress reactions. *Work Stress, 18*, 336–351.

Aquino, K., & Thau, S. (2009). Workplace victimization: Aggression from the target's perspective. *Annual Review of Psychology, 60*, 717–741.

Ashcraft, C. (2000). Naming knowledge: A language for reconstructing domestic violence and systemic gender inequity. *Women and Language, 23*, 3–10.

Ashforth, B. E., & Humphrey, R. H. (1993). Emotional labor in service roles: The influence of identity. *Academy of Management Review, 18*, 88–115.

Baba, V. V., Galperin, B. L., & Lituchy, T. R. (1999). Occupational mental health: A study of work-related depression among nurses in the Caribbean. *International Journal of Nursing Studies, 36*, 163–169.

Berkowitz, L. (1993). *Aggression: Its causes, consequences, and control*. New York: McGraw-Hill.

Bies, R. J. (2000). Interactional (in)justice: The sacred and the profane. In J. Greenberg & R. Cropanzano (Eds.), *Advances in organizational behavior*. San Francisco: New Lexington Press.

Bies, R. J., & Moag, J. S. (1986). Interactional justice: Communications criteria of fairness. In R. Lewicki & B. Sheppard (Eds.), *Research on negotiation in organizations* (Vol. 1, pp. 43–55). Greenwich: JAI Press.

Bies, R. J., & Tripp, T. M. (1996). Beyond distrust: Getting even and the need for revenge. In R. M. Kramer & T. Tyler (Eds.), *Trust and organizations* (pp. 246–260). Thousand Oaks: Sage.

Carpenter, J. (1995). Doctors and nurses: Stereotypes and stereotype change in interprofessional education. *Journal of Interprofessional Care, 9*, 151–161.

Caza, B. B., & Cortina, L. M. (2007). From insult to injury: Explaining the impact of incivility. *Basic and Applied Social Psychology, 29*, 335–350.

Chiaburu, D. S., & Harrison, D. A. (2008). Do peers make the place? Conceptual synthesis and meta-analysis of co-worker effects on perceptions, attitudes, OCBs and performance. *Journal of Applied Psychology, 93*, 1082–1103.

Choi, B. C. K., & Pak, A. W. P. (2006). Multidisciplinarity, interdisciplinarity and transdisciplinarity in health research, services, education and policy: 1. Definitions, objectives, and evidence of effectiveness. *Clinical Investigatory Medicine, 29*, 351–364.

Cook, J., & Wall, T. (1980). New work attitude measures of trust, organizational commitment and personal need non-fulfillment. *Journal of Occupational Psychology, 53*, 39–52.

Cortina, L. M. (2008). Unseen injustice: Incivility as modern discrimination in organizations. *Academy of Management Review, 33*, 55–57.

Cortina, L. M., Magley, V. J., Williams, J. H., & Langhout, R. D. (2001). Incivility in the workplace: Incidence and impact. *Journal of Occupational Health Psychology, 6*, 64–80.

Cowen, R. L. (2011). Yes, we have an anti-bullying policy, but … : HR Professionals' understandings and experiences with workplace bullying policy. *Communication Studies, 62*, 307–327.

Crocker, J., & Major, B. (1989). Social stigma and self-esteem: The self-protective properties of stigma. *Psychological Review, 96*, 608–630.

Crocker, J., Voelkl, K., Testa, M., & Major, B. (1991). Social stigma: The affective consequences of attributional ambiguity. *Journal of Personality and Social Psychology, 60*, 218–228.

Daniel, T. A. (2006). Bullies in the workplace: A focus on the abusive disrespect of employees. *Society for Human Resource Management*. Retrieved January 21, 2012, from http://thepeoplegroupllc.com/wp-content/uploads/2008/04/article-bullies-in-the-workplace.pdf.

Davenport, N., Schwartz, R., & Elliott, G. P. (1999). *Mobbing: Emotional abuse in the workplace*. Ames: Civil Society Publishing.

Douglas, S. C., & Martinko, M. J. (2001). Exploring the role of individual differences in the prediction of workplace aggression. *Journal of Applied Psychology, 86*, 547–559.

Edmondson, A. (1999). Psychological safety and learning behavior in work teams. *Administrative Science Quarterly, 44*, 350–383.

Gilin-Oore, D., LeBlanc, D., Day, A., Leiter, M. P., Laschinger, H. K. S., Price, S. L., Latimer, M. (2010). When respect deteriorates: Incivility as a moderator of the stressor-strain relationship among hospital workers. *Journal of Nursing Management, 18*, 878–888.

Glasø, L., Nielsen, M. B., & Einarsen, S. (2009). Interpersonal problems among perpetrators and targets of workplace bullying. *Journal of Applied Social Psychology, 39*, 1316–1333.

Grandey, A. A., Kern, J. H., & Frone, M. R. (2007). Verbal abuse from outsiders versus insiders: Comparing frequency, impact on emotional exhaustion, and the role of emotional labor. *Journal of Occupational and Health Psychology, 12*(1), 63–79.

Halbesleben, J. R. B. (2006). Sources of social support and burnout: A meta-analytic test of the conservation of resources model. *Journal of Applied Psychology, 91*, 1134–1145.

Hansen, A. M., Hogh, A., Persson, R., Karlson, B., Garde, A. H., & Orbaek, P. (2006). Bullying at work, health outcomes, and physiological stress response. *Journal of Psychosomatic Research, 60*, 63–72.

Harthill, S. (2008). Bullying in the workpalce: Lessons from the United Kingdom. *Minnesota Journal of International Law, 17*, 247–253.

Harvey, M. G., Heames, J. T., Richey, R. G., & Leonard, N. (2006). Bullying: From the playground to the boardroom. *Journal of Leadership and Organizational Studies, 12*(4), 1–11.

Hauge, L. J., Skogstad, A., & Einarsen, S. L. (2010). The relative impact of workplace bullying as a social stressor at work. *Scandinavian Journal of Psychology, 51*, 426–433.

Hershcovis, M. S., & Barling, J. (2010). Comparing victim attributions and outcomes for workplace aggression and sexual harassment. *Journal of Applied Psychology, 95*, 874–888.

Isaac, C. A. (2011). Women leaders: The social world of health care. *Journal of Health Organization and Management, 25*, 159–175.

Keashly, L., Hunter, S., & Harvey, S. (1997). Abusive interaction and role state stressors: Relative impact on student residence assistant stress and work attitudes. *Work and Stress, 11*, 175–185.

Kets de Vries, M. F. R. (1985). The dark side of entrepreneurship. *Harvard Business Review, 63*(6), 160–167.

Kivimaki, M., Elovainio, M., & Vahtera, J. (2000). Workplace bullying and sickness absence in hospital staff. *Occupational and Environmental Medicine, 57*, 656–660.

Kramer, R. M. (1999). Trust and distrust in organizations: Emerging perspectives, enduring questions. *Annual Review of Psychology, 50*, 569–598.

Laschinger, H. K. S., & Finegan, J. E. (2005). Using empowerment to build trust and respect in the workplace: A strategy for addressing the nursing shortage. *Nursing Economics, 23*, 6–13.

LeBlanc, M. M., & Kelloway, E. K. (2002). Predictors and outcomes of workplace violence and aggression. *Journal of Applied Psychology, 87*, 444–453.

Leiter, M. P., Laschinger, H. K. S., Day, A., & Gilin-Oore, D. (2011). The impact of civility interventions on employee social behavior, distress, and attitudes. *Journal of Applied Psychology, 96*, 1258–1274.

Leiter, M. P., & Maslach, C. (1988). The impact of interpersonal environment on burnout and organizational commitment. *Journal of Organizational Behavior, 9*, 297–308.

Leiter, M. P., & Maslach, C. (2009). Nurse turnover: The mediating role of burnout. *Journal of Nursing Management, 17*, 331–339.

Leiter, M. P., & Stright, N. (2009). The social context of work life: Implications for burnout and work engagement. In C. L. Cooper, J. C. Quick, & M. J. Schabracq (Eds.), *International handbook of work and health psychology* (3rd ed.) (pp. 25–47). Chichester: Wiley.

Leiter, M. P., Price, S. L., & Laschinger, H. K. S. (2010). Generational differences in distress, attitudes and incivility among nurses. *Journal of Nursing Management, 18*, 970–980.

Liang, S.-C., & Hsieh, A.-T. (2008). The role of organizational socialization in burnout: A Taiwanese example. *Social Behavior and Personality, 36*, 197–216.

Lim, S., & Lee, A. (2011). Work and nonwork outcomes of workplace incivility: Does family support help? *Journal of Occupational Health Psychology, 16*(1), 95–111.

Lopez, S. H., Hodson, R., & Roscigno, V. J. (2009). Power, status, and abuse at work: General and sexual harassment compared. *Sociological Quarterly, 50*, 3–27.

Lutgen-Sandvik, P. (2008). Intensive remedial identity work: Responses to workplace bullying trauma and stigmatization. *Organization, 15*, 97–119.

MacKay, L. (1992). Nursing and doctoring: Where's the difference. In K. Soothill, C. Henry, & C. Kendrick (Eds.) *Interprofessional relations in health care*. London: Edward Arnold.

Maslach, C., & Leiter, M. P. (2008). Early predictors of job burnout and engagement. *Journal of Applied Psychology, 93*, 498–512.

Matthiesen, S. B., & Einarsen, S. (2007). Perpetrators and targets of bullying at work: Role stress and individual differences. *Violence and Victims, 22*, 735–753.

Meglich, P. A., & Eesley, D. T. (2011). A bully in its own China shop: Risk factors for abusive supervision in small firms. *International Journal of Business and Social Science, 2*, 11–22.

Mills, S. (2009). Impoliteness in a cultural context. *Journal of Pragmatics, 41*, 1047–1060. http://dx.doi.org/10.1016/j.pragma.2008.10.014.

O'Moore, M., & Lynch, J. (2007). Leadership, working environment and workplace bullying. *International Journal of Organization Theory and Behavior, 10*(1), 95–117.

Pearson, C., Andersson, L., & Porath, C. (2005). Workplace incivility. In S. Fox & P. E. Spector (Eds.), *Counterproductive work behavior: Investigations of actors and targets*. Washington: American Psychological Association.

Pearson, C., & Porath, C. (2009). *The cost of bad behavior: How incivility is damaging your business and what to do about it*. New York: Penguin Books.

Semmer, N., & Schallberger, U. (1996). Selection, socialization, and mutual adaptation: Resolving discrepancies between people and their work. *Applied Psychology: An International Review, 45*, 263–288.

Skarlicki, D. P., & Folger, R. (1997). Retaliation in the workplace: The roles of distributive, procedural, and interactional justice. *Journal of Applied Psychology, 82*, 434–443.

Skogstad, A., Einarsen, S., Torsheim, T., Aasland, M. S., & Hetland, H. (2007). The destructiveness of laissez-faire leadership behavior. *Journal of Occupational Health Psychology, 12*, 80–92.

Sonnentag, S., Mojza, E., & Binnewies, C. (2010). Staying well and engaged when demands are high: The role of psychological detachment. *Journal of Applied Psychology, 95*, 965–976.

Spreitzer, G. M. (1995). Individual empowerment in the workplace: Dimensions, measurement, and validation. *Academy of Management Journal, 38*, 1442–1465.

Stone, K. L. (2009). From queen bees and wannabes to worker bees: Why gender considerations should inform the emerging law of workplace bullying. *New York University Annual Survey of American Law, 35*, 52–53.

Tepper, B. J. (2000). Consequences of abusive supervision. *Academy of Management Journal, 43*, 178–190.

Trudel, J. (2010). *Workplace incivility: Relationship with conflict management styles and impact on perceived job performance, organizational commitment and turnover.* Ph.D. dissertation, University of Louisville, United States—Kentucky. Retrieved November 5, 2010, from Dissertations & Theses: Full Text (Publication No. AAT 3381935).

Walter, F., & Bruch, H. (2008). The positive group affect spiral: A dynamic model of the emergence of positive affective similarity in work groups. *Journal of Organizational Behavior, 29*, 239–261.

Wenger, E. (1998). *Communities of practice*. Cambridge: Cambridge University Press.

Wilson, V., & Pirrie, A. (2000). *Multidisciplinary teamworking—beyond the barriers? A review of the issues*. Edinburgh: SCRE.

Yamada, D. (2000). The phenomenon of workplace bullying and the need for status-blind hostile work environment protection. *Georgetown Law Journal, 88*, 475–536.

Chapter 4
Taking Action to Address Workplace Incivility

Abstract This chapter considers strategies for improving civility among members of workgroups. It begins with noting the challenges inherent in changing civility in light of the social embedded nature of the construct. The chapter considers three qualities that facilitate change: (1) creating a psychologically safe environment (2) structuring the process to encourage reflection upon one's own behavior and that of others, and (3) using a shared group process rather than individual treatment. The chapter considers the scope of individual and management interventions to address civility and incivility challenges.

Taking Action: What Improves the Quality of Working Relationships?

Improving civility at work is a challenge. The research literature is replete with suggestions for taking action, but only a few studies have rigorously tested procedures. Books and websites offer advice that reflect the authors' perspective on workplace mistreatment, but lack rigorous evaluation of their suggestions effectiveness (Alkon 2009; Truss 2005). They include the effectiveness of their suggestions for individuals on ways to respond to bullies and advice to bystanders on how to be helpful (Namie and Lutgen-Sandvik 2010). Research articles have speculated on how general principles of workgroup change can apply to addressing incivility. Questionnaire research has identified correlations of various constructs with civility or incivility leading to suggestions to improve civility. At present, research has only begun to establish evidence-based principles for improving workplace civility. Much work remains.

Understanding the causes and impact of workplace mistreatment is one step in a process towards taking action to address the problem. At this point in the development

M. Leiter, *Analyzing and Theorizing the Dynamics of the Workplace Incivility Crisis*, SpringerBriefs in Psychology,
DOI: 10.1007/978-94-007-5571-0_4, © The Author(s) 2013

of this field, researchers have sufficient information to take action. It is unlikely that an increasingly fine-grained analysis of the subtle factors distinguishing forms of mistreatment will produce a perfect intervention design. It is more likely that progress on improving the impact of interventions will occur through testing procedures, noting their strengths and weaknesses, and adjusting the process in subsequent tests. The field calls out for research projects that take action and closely monitor how events unfold.

Increasing Civility is a Challenging Learning Objective

People are slow to change the way they interact with colleagues day-to-day, even when dedicated, well-educated people see the error of their ways and the benefits of change. Civility shares this paradox with other important behaviors. An example that has received attention that includes large-scale intervention is hand washing among hospital physicians. Although physicians are well-educated health care practitioners who universally subscribe to the germ theory of disease, they have a less than impressive record at washing their hands between patient contacts. Attempts to improve hand washing rates have found it to be an uphill battle. One approach found success with a mixture of disgust and salience. Porzig-Drummond et al. (2009) took bacterial cultures of hospital physicians' hands, gave the culture a few days to evolve, vividly stained the various strains of bacteria to produce a map of the physicians' hand. The more definitive images were distributed as screen savers on the hospital's computer system. This intervention had a definitive impact on improving hand washing among physicians. However, the authors noted that they expected that no intervention would be effective forever; innovative strategies would be needed to maintain their gains.

A lesson from this work to inform efforts to improve civility is that interventions are more effective when they address the irrational dimensions of established behaviors. That is, people do not behave uncivilly only because they do not know how to act. Otherwise rational people initiate behaviors that make no sense and other sensible people react to them irrationally. A lesson from the hand washing study is simply providing a bit more information about civil behavior is unlikely to suffice. An effective intervention will present accurate, evidence-based information in ways that have a compelling quality.

The discussion of intervention approaches begins with reflecting on the necessary conditions to encourage change. These conditions include:

- Creating a Psychologically Safe Environment
- Encouraging a Reflective Process
- Supporting Shared Efforts for a Broad Impact

Each of these conditions has a foundation in current theories and research about workplace mistreatment and teamwork. The following section explores each quality and its rationale.

Condition One: Creating a Psychologically Safe Environment

Proposition 4: Improving Civility Benefits from Psychological Safety

Even when in distressing circumstances, people hesitate to embrace opportunities for change. "Better the devil you know," is an often heard statement from people enduring hard circumstances or difficult bosses. When feeling seriously at risk, minimizing one's losses seems to take priority over improving one's circumstances.

Frederickson's (2001) Broaden and Build model provides a constructive perspective on the change process. The model shares features with the Risk Management Model in its consideration of employees' concern with the riskiness of their environment. Frederickson contends that stress reduces employees' perspectives on their situations. The biological underpinnings of the human stress response narrow one's focus on a specific threat while generating anxiety that motivates a fight or flight response. In risky circumstances, survival needs encourage people to do what they have already mastered. If they are good at fighting, they fight; if they can run fast, they run; if they are good at hiding, they hide. The dominant theme of demand situations is executing one's existing repertoire of skills as effectively as possible. They resort to familiar strategies, reducing their capacity for creative problem solving.

In contrast, learning occurs more readily when people feel safe. Supportive, empowering experiences at work broaden their perspective. Without the pressure to respond to external demands, intrinsic priorities become increasingly relevant.

Edmondson (1999) proposed a key condition for learning is a sense of psychological safety. The workgroup plays a pivotal role in determining employees' sense of psychological safety. A psychologically safe workgroup is one in which members feel confident that they would receive a positive response from other group members if they should raise tough issues for discussion. Rather than increasing employees' sense of risk, the psychologically safe workgroup actively supports its members when they embark on new or uncertain activities. In such an environment people are more likely to learn and to bring creativity to their work.

The importance of safety for learning presents an immediate challenge in promoting civility: to the extent that a worksetting lacks civility, it is a risky environment. Its riskiness gives the workgroup the qualities that discourage learning. The process of learning a new skill begins with an awkward phase. The initial forays into a new mode of interaction are unlikely to be smoothly executed. People learning to play the violin are usually tentative in the first occasions when they perform for an audience. Learning new ways to interact socially shares that tentative quality. At work people would rather convey a sense of competence, especially in something so basic as how they interact with their colleagues and their boss. The fear of trying something new may be greater than the discomfort of enduring the status quo. In contrast, Edmondson (2004) noted that learning occurs when the anxiety associated with the status quo is greater than the anxiety arising from the risk of looking incompetent to colleagues. She pointed out that anxiety has been long identified as undermining organizational attempts to improve cultures and establish new standards of behavior (Argyris 1990; Schein 1995). "A face-to-face work team can provide a safety net for learning, or, in contrast, be a place where the risk of learning behavior is magnified" (Edmondson 2004, p. 28). Learning workplace civility magnifies this risk because the focus of learning is precisely the quality that defines the risk inherent in a team.

This condition defines the first task in establishing psychological safety to improve workplace civility. At a minimum, the intervention will define a time and place that is safe to experiment with new ways of interacting. In these sessions the facilitators make a concerted and consistent effort to maintain discourse free of harsh criticism or personal attacks.

Psychological safety may be a necessary but it is certainly not a sufficient condition for learning. Although the environment presents fewer risks, team members may be content to remain with the status quo. Learning still requires either dissatisfaction with the status quo or an active desire to work towards a meaningful goal.

Condition Two: Encouraging a Reflective Process

Proposition 5: Improving Civility Requires a Reflective Process

The discussion in Chap. 1 contrasting empathy with emotional contagion argued for a reflective process to improve the quality of relationships among colleagues. The sensitivity of people to the emotional states of those around them builds connections but it does so in ways that perpetuate the existing quality of community. Initiating change in the ongoing flow of dialogue requires people to empathize with their colleagues' expectations for respect, their vulnerabilities to mistreatment, and their hopes for fulfilling relationships.

The immediate benefit of empathy is its incompatibility with thoughtlessness. Taking another person's perspective requires focused attention and imagination. In other words, taking the other person's perspective into consideration takes a concerted effort, because empathy requires a distinct focus on the way another person perceives a situation. The other person becomes more than a one-dimensional element within one's world. The other person becomes the defining perspective for evaluating the situation. A qualitative analysis of health care providers' interviews demonstrated that failures to establish empathy with patients occur when providers limit their focus on the patient as an information source. Moving beyond superficial details to focus on patients' motivational issues encourages active patient participation in treatment (Pillai 2010). Seymour (2004) makes a strong case for empathy playing a central role in nursing. Hope-Stone and Mills (2001) reported that nurses understand empathy as combining their professional and personal contact with patients to reflect a combination of analytical and emotional perspectives. Wiseman (1996) emphasized the emotional quality of empathy in a concept analysis of the term. Goldie (1999) made a distinction between empathy and sympathy with the latter focused on feeling distress about another person's experience. Empathy has more of a quality of imagining a story in which the other person is the central character. Wiseman (1996), consistent with Goldie, argues that self-awareness is a fundamental building block for empathy as it permits people to separate their own emotional state from that of the other person. It is necessary to maintain an emotional distance in order to appreciate fully another person's perspective.

Seymour and Ingleton (2004) acknowledge that empathy has inherent risks as it increases nurses‘ emotional vulnerability. For example, Degner et al. (1991) included in a list of seven critical nursing behaviors for palliative care, "Responding to anger: showing respect and empathy even when anger is directed at the nurse" (Seymour and Ingleton, 2004, p. 200). The capacity to work past the emotional impact of another person‘s anger to establish empathy requires an exceptional level confidence. Accepting the additional risk of empathy is especially challenging when people feel already at risk in an uncivil workplace. From the perspective of the Risk Management Model a mutually supportive team will provide a more solid base for the level of confidence necessary to show empathy in one‘s work.

Condition Three: Supporting Shared Efforts for a Broad Impact

Civility and incivility are shared events. Although people can shape their social behavior to influence the behavior of other people, progress comes more smoothly when people work together to improve their relationships from both sides of an interaction. Extensive research on family therapy has made this point repeatedly (Szapocznik and Williams 2000). Simply put, it is much easier to behave civilly when others are doing their best to behave civilly. It reduces the effort required to resist the temptation to retaliate against bad behavior. A shared effort to change relationships has much more leverage than a lone person hoping to resist the current of social discourse. When things go off track, it is possible to talk with one another about an incident rather than to smolder with unresolved resentment.

A group initiative recognizes workplace culture as a shared responsibility and a shared resource. Within a strong culture the interactions among members of a workgroup reflect its core values. Generally, egalitarian inclusive groups show a stronger commitment to mutual respect in contrast to groups with a strong sense of hierarchy or an in-group/out-group dynamic (Cortina 2008). Difficulties are acute when the espoused values conflict with values-in-action, creating risk in the organizational environment (Argyris 1990). Within a group that espouses respectful working relationships but falls short of realizing that value, life becomes especially strained for low status members. They directly experience the gap between espoused and realized values, but lack the capacity to challenge the state of affairs. When a group is working together to improve their workplace culture, even low status members have the capacity to call their colleagues to account for their behavior.

In many situations, low status members have the greatest motivation for change—they feel most at risk in the group's social environment—but they have the least power to effect change. A unilateral change in low status members' behavior will not be compelling. They may react differently to a harsh statement from a colleague, but others ignore the change in their behavior. However, by working together, group members can establish new sequences of social behavior. Even if new behaviors seem artificial at first, a pattern emerges. For example, one initiative that can change the tone of a workgroup culture is expressing appreciation to colleagues. An individual may express thanks without causing more than a minor ripple in the group's interaction. A group of colleagues working together can follow up one another's expression of appreciation with comments that reinforce the statements, making it a more resonate part of the workgroup. These conversations help to embed appreciation as a core element of the workgroup's culture.

Incivility—whether intended or unintended—arises from separate sources as each party has its distinct culture giving a special status to its members over others. No party can single-handedly overcome the resulting culture plagued by miscommunication, service gaps, and turf battles among people who disagree about one another's proper role. The problem does not reside within any one individual or group; the problem resides between them.

Intervention Formats

Individual Interventions

Bullying has become a pervasive meme in contemporary culture in 2012, prompting various parties to offer solutions on the individual level. They direct their advice to the recipients of mistreatment. Suggestions include emotion-focused coping (managing one's emotional reaction to a mistreatment incident) as well as action-focused coping (steps to take to prevent further mistreatment). For example, the advice from the Workplace Bullying Institute (http://www.workplacebullying.org/individuals/solutions/wbi-action-plan/) combines advice on formal complaint processes combined with strategies for maintaining positive self-esteem while enduring and attempting to address bullying. The general perspective of anti-bullying champions is that (1) some flawed individuals are inherently bullies who will continue to mistreat others until forced to stop by a greater power (2) bullies single out low power individuals to victimize, and (3) appeals to high power individuals or groups (in terms of management authority, legal standing, or knowledge) play a role in rectifying the bullying/victim relationship. These approaches frame the issue in terms of the psychopathology of the bully and the distress of the victim. They make few references to the workplace culture or to shared responsibility for unpleasant encounters at work. Some sites advise confronting the bully (e. g., http://humanresources.about.com/od/difficultpeople/qt/work_bully.htm) while others avoid direct confrontation while documenting the bullying behavior as evidence. This approach is relevant when there are strong organizational policies or legislative solutions to address workplace mistreatment.

The overwhelming majority of resources on bullying provide advice to victims rather than to perpetrators. Individual interventions for perpetrators are less common, but are available. Some strive to improve social behavior towards others at work. They include emotion-focused programs, such as anger management. Other approaches take an information-based focus, such as contemporary etiquette books or workshops (e. g., Langford 2005; Post and Post 2005) that describe codes of behavior that reduce the probability of unintentionally offending others. The Slate.com series, Manners for the Digital Age (http://www.slate.com/articles/podcasts/manners_for_the_digital_age.html) provides a series of conversations on etiquette issues in a podcast format. Langlois (2012) gives five suggestions for improving conversations among nurses on critical care wards. Another example was on the BBC website on a story regarding email bullying: (BBC 2003: http://news.bbc.co.uk/2/hi/technology/2902777.stm).

Start box

"HOW TO AVOID BEING A BULLY

Do not write e-mails in capital letters
Put some pleasantries in your e-mail
Communicate face to face with people sitting near you
Use copy fields sparingly and appropriately
Sarcasm does not work in e-mails
Never write anything you would not like to see stored by your company
Reflect on what you have written before sending"

End Box

To date, there are no published research studies evaluating the efficacy of individual approaches. There are anecdotal descriptions of individuals who have found such advice helpful but little information on the number of people who attempt to resolve matters in line with the advice.

Management Interventions to Improve Workplace Civility

Management interventions frame the problem of incivility as a system challenge rather than simply an individual failing. First, a well-managed organization needs policies and procedures that respond to instances of mistreatment among employees. Individuals do behave badly or even violently; organizations need to respond effectively. The primary objective is to reduce the incident, frequency, and intensity of bad behavior. Second, management interventions include programs for improving workplace communities. These initiatives may occur in response to identified problems within workgroups or be generally applied regardless of whether participating groups have identified mistreatment as an issue. Both types of intervention acknowledge social behavior among employees as a legitimate management issue.

The research literature provides a few, but very few, instances of rigorously tested organizational interventions to improve civility or to reduce mistreatment. One exception that the following two chapters explore is CREW: Civility, Respect, and Engagement at Work. Chapter 5 presents CREW's development within the Veterans Health Administration. Chapter 6 presents its evaluation in Canadian hospitals. Research on CREW has the qualities of pretest, post-test, and follow-up assessments for intervention and control groups. They depart from experimental design in that participants are not randomly assigned and they are generally aware of the research goals. These departures from experimental design are a necessary part of conducting research within hospitals whose primary concern is the quality of patient care. Ethical standards in organizational research demand that participants be informed of research programs. The departures from strict experimental design bring the benefit of increasing the studies' external validity by approximating more closely the conditions under which a hospital would implement the process: they would apply CREW to units with an identified need (not randomly) and they would inform participants about the purpose of the process.

Another approach for management intervention is developing and monitoring policies to assure civil, respectful workplaces. Pearson and Porath (2009) proposed a series of management actions and policies to reduce workplace incivility:

1. A zero tolerance for workplace mistreatment: Management needs to act decisively in response to incidents.
2. Leaders would benefit from self-reflection on the civility or incivility reflected in their own behavior.
3. Employees would benefit from management buffering them from uncivil behavior from customers.
4. Actively promote and instruct civil behavior as part of professional development and orientation programs.
5. First line managers would benefit from training on interrupting incivility spirals in their workgroups.
6. Organizations need ongoing systems for thoroughly investigating employee claims of mistreatment.
7. Management would be informed by employee surveys that assess workplace civility as well as other aspects of worklife.
8. Prompt reactions to reported incidents of incivility builds credibility for management's commitment to community values.
9. A strong culture of civility does not accept the legitimacy of any excuses for incivility.
10. Exit interviews help to identify the extent to which workplace incivility influences employees' turnover decisions.

Together these recommendations provide a comprehensive consideration of management action to reinforce the salience of respect as an organizational value.

Establishing ongoing policies and procedures assure that they continue beyond the scope of individual leaders. They become part of the fabric of the organization.

Conclusion

The problems of mistreatment at work have prompted advice on ways of improving working relationships or workplace culture. Some advice approaches mistreatment as an individual problem of people who misuse authority or physical power to intimidate dis-empowered colleagues. Other advice approaches mistreatment as a breakdown in workplace culture. The advice generally works from an assumption that existing management approaches to addressing workplace mistreatment are ineffective if not damaging to the complainants.

A major shortcoming in the thinking about intervention is the small amount of research that has objectively evaluated interventions, comparing their impact to what happens in control groups. The following two chapters examine two research programs that have evaluated an organizational approach to improving workplace civility. This approach views workplace mistreatments as a breakdown in organizational culture and seeks to facilitate team members to improve that culture.

References

Alkon, A. (2009). *I see rude people: One woman's battle to beat some manners into impolite society*. New York: McGraw-Hill.

Argyris, C. (1990). *Overcoming organizational defenses: Facilitating organizational learning*. Boston: Allyn and Bacon.

BBC, (2003). *E-mail bullying on the rise*. Posted 31 March, 2003. Retrieved February 29, 2012, http://news.bbc.co.uk/2/hi/technology/2902777.stm.

Cortina, L. M. (2008). Unseen injustice: Incivility as modern discrimination in organizations. *Academy of Management Review, 33*, 55–57.

Degner, L. F., Gow, C. M., & Thompson, L. A. (1991). Critical nursing behaviours in care of the dying. *Cancer Nursing, 14*, 246–253.

Edmondson, A. (1999). Psychological safety and learning behavior in work teams. *Administrative Science Quarterly, 44*, 350–383.

Edmondson, A. (2004). Psychological safety, trust, and learning in organizations: A group lens. In R. M. Kramer & K. S. Cook (Eds.), *Trust and distrust in organizations: Dilemmas and approaches* (pp. 239–272). New York: Russell Sage.

Fredrickson, B. L. (2001). The role of positive emotions in positive psychology: The broaden-and-build theory of positive emotions. *American Psychologist, 56*, 218–226.

Goldie, P. (1999). How we think of others' emotions. *Mind and Language, 14*, 394–423.

Hope-Stone, L. D., & Mills, B. (2001). Developing empathy to improve patient care: A pilot study of cancer nurses. *International Journal of Palliative Nursing, 7*, 146–150.

Langford, B. (2005). *The etiquette edge: The unspoken rules for business success*. New York: AMACOM Books.

Langlois, B. (2012). Five steps to reduce bullying. *Nursing Critical Care, 7*, 48.

Namie, G., & Lutgen-Sandvik, P. (2010). Active and passive accomplices: The communal character of workplace bullying. *International Journal of Communication, 4*, 354.
Pearson, C., & Porath, C. (2009). *The cost of bad Behavior: How incivility is damaging your business and what to do about it*. New York: Penguin Books.
Pillai, A. K. (2010). *Use of empathy by healthcare professionals learning motivational interviewing: A qualitative analysis*. Thesis. Auburn University, Auburn, Alabama.
Porzig-Drummond, R., Stevenson, R., Case, T., & Oaten, M. (2009). Can the emotion of disgust be harnessed to promote hand hygiene? Experimental and field-based tests. *Social Science and Medicine, 68*, 1006–1012.
Post, P. & Post, P. (2005). *The etiquette advantage in business*. New York: Harper Collins.
Schein, E. (1995). *Kurt Lewin's change theory in the field and in the classroom: Notes toward a model of managed learning*. Working Paper. Available at http://www.a2zpsychology.com/articles/kurt_lewin's_change_theory.htm.
Seymour, J. (2004). What's in a name? A concept analysis of key terms in palliative care nursing. In S. Payne, J. Seymour, & C. Ingleton (Eds.), *Palliative care nursing: Principles and evidence for practice* (pp. 55–71). Berkshire: Open University Press.
Seymour, J., & Ingleton, C. (2004). Overview: Transitions into the terminal phase. In S. Payne, J. Seymour, & C. Ingleton (Eds.), *Palliative care nursing: Principles and evidence for practice* (pp. 189–217). Berkshire: Open University Press.
Szapocznik, J., & Williams, R. A. (2000). Brief strategic family therapy: Twenty-five years of interplay among theory, research and practice in adolescent behavior problems and drug abuse. *Clinical Child and Family Psychology Review, 3*, 117–134.
Truss, L. (2005). *Talk to the hand: The utter bloody rudeness of the world today, or six good reasons to stay home and bolt the door*. New York: Gotham.
Wiseman, T. (1996). Listening and empathy: A concept analysis of empathy. *Journal of Advanced Nursing, 23*, 1162–1167.

Chapter 5
Civility, Respect, and Engagement (CREW) in the Workplace at the Veterans Health Administration

Abstract This chapter discusses an intervention that promotes civil climate within organizations, designed within the USA Veterans Health Administration and called Civility, Respect, and Engagement in the Workplace (CREW). *Civility* in the CREW model refers to workplace behaviors that express interpersonally valuing and being valued by others, and are based on a consciously cultivated awareness of one's interpersonal impact. CREW process within groups involves regular meetings that create opportunities for an ongoing dialogue where participants clarify and negotiate their understanding of group norms for civil interactions at work. The content of workplace behaviors considered civil is culturally specific to each workplace and is therefore defined by the participating groups themselves, a practice which results in an intentional (conceptually driven) variability in interpreting what constitutes civil behaviors across sites. We discuss the implications of this variability for designing and studying CREW interventions, understanding the mechanisms of change in CREW, and evaluating outcomes.

Veterans Hospital Administration

A great deal has been written about the negative impact of incivility and its costs to organizations, but less is known about how to counteract it by establishing a civil workplace climate. Like others (e.g., Pearson et al. 2005), we believe that promoting civility at the workplace may work best at the organizational rather than at

---

Civility, Respect, and Engagement in the Workplace (CREW): An intervention promoting positive organizational culture
Katerine Osatuke, Sue Dyrenforth & Linda Belton
National Center for Organizational Development
Veterans Hospital Administration

M. Leiter, *Analyzing and Theorizing the Dynamics of the Workplace Incivility Crisis*, SpringerBriefs in Psychology,
DOI: 10.1007/978-94-007-5571-0_5,

the purely individual level. This is because instances of civility and incivility are all manifestations of a broader interactive process that happens within a specific context (e.g. a workgroup, an entire organization) rather than single static events occurring between separate people (Pearson et al. 2005; Osatuke et al. 2009). This chapter discusses an intervention that promotes civil climate within organizations. A detailed description of how the civility-focused intervention proceeds along with empirical evidence for successful outcomes have been presented elsewhere (Osatuke et al. 2009; Leiter et al. 2011). In this chapter, we share the conceptual rationale for this approach, describe how these concepts inform the main features of the intervention, and explain to what we attribute its demonstrated success.

The intervention called Civility, Respect, and Engagement in the Workplace (CREW) was initially designed by the National Center of Organization Development within the USA Veterans Health Administration (VHA), with support and participation of top VHA leaders. CREW grew out of a need identified by the VHA to attend to the organizational culture of everyday interactions at work. The top VHA leaders' commitment to enhancing this area of organizational life reflected a growing understanding within VA (e.g. Young 2000) and, on a broader scale. Within the US government sector (e.g. The United States Postal Service Commission 2000) that civility is a crucial part of the organizational climate perceived by employees. As such, civility influences not only individual employee outcomes (such as levels of organizational commitment and job satisfaction) but also higher level outcomes directly connected to the organizational mission, including quality of patient care, operational costs, ability to retain quality workforce, and others. VHA leaders considered results from several internal studies (see Osatuke et al. 2009 for a more detailed review), all pointing to an area of concern about civility, or how we treat one another within the organization. This concern resulted in a pilot of a new initiative aimed at improving civil and respectful interactions within VHA, both between management and employees and between peers.

Civility is the key concept in CREW. Our basic understanding of this term encompasses attitudes and behaviors that express interpersonally valuing and being valued by others. This understanding is consistent with previous definitions of civility in organization development (OD) and industrial-organizational (IO) psychology (e.g. Anderson and Pearson 1999). It reflects a long-standing line of thinking that emphasized the importance of related concepts in the life of workers and organizations (e.g. Adlerfer 1972; Argyris 1964; Herzberg et al. 1959; Likert 1961; Maslow 1973; Rogers 1977). In addition to this basic definition, *civility* in the VHA CREW model is more specifically understood as on-stage workplace behaviors, based on a consciously cultivated awareness of one's interpersonal impact. This awareness comes with the organization's expectation of the individual to monitor their own behavior during interpersonal interactions, pay attention to how other people receive it, and modify the behavior if necessary (that is, if its immediate interpersonal outcomes were unintended). Within the CREW intervention model, civil behaviors are seen as impersonal (displayed on behalf of the organization), and directed toward *everyone* at the workplace, rather than only toward people one knows. For example, a greeting of "hello" to a passerby or holding the door open for another is a civil, rather than personal behavior.

Providing *organizational support for civility* constitutes the first element of the CREW model as it was designed within VHA. When present, such support is reflected in employees' perceptions that their organization consistently enforces civil workplace behaviors—for example, through organizational policies, management strategies, and specific supervisors' behaviors towards subordinates. Organizational support for civility is expected to impact workplace perceptions, making employees feel *respected*; this constitutes the second element of the model. These perceptions, in turn, are expected to empower employee actions at the workplace, resulting in greater *engagement* (the third element of the model) into collaborative efforts toward the organization's shared goals. These expectations, generally consistent with previous organization development thinking (e.g. Ostroff 1992) and existing research (e.g. Laschinger and Finegan 2005; Parker et al. 2003), were based on VHA leaders' interpretation of results from internal studies. They formed the basis of the VHA CREW approach and represented a broad operational context for planning and implementing CREW interventions.

The first application of CREW in 2005 proved highly successful, prompting its quick spread, first within VHA and then across the entire USA Department of Veterans Affairs (VA). The CREW model has been freely shared with interested organizations. As a result, by the present time, several non-VA organizations including those within and outside the USA, in government and in private sectors, in healthcare as well as in other industries, have successfully implemented the VHA CREW model.

The overarching purpose of CREW is to raise awareness of the importance of civility and respect in the workplace. When an intervention starts, this overarching purpose typically translates into conversations about how workplace civility helps achieve the organizational mission (that is, making the business case for civility for this specific unit). Participants also discuss and ultimately come to an agreement about what defines a respectful workplace in their particular unit or team. They jointly identify barriers or bad habits that get in the way of creating a respectful workplace, and establish commitment to the common goal of "raising the bar" for civility norms (acceptable workplace behaviors). As CREW progresses, groups focus on maintaining awareness of the climate within the unit with regard to respect and civility. Follow-up activities also include engaging all staff in recognizing and rewarding those behaviors which, in the intervention participants' agreement, improve the workplace climate. The CREW activities in given groups are linked to other values, priorities, and aspects of work and culture within the organization. Groups also highlight and celebrate the outcomes of their improved climate.

Of note, the specific content of workplace behaviors that are considered civil is not part of the CREW model; instead, it is defined locally, on a case-per-case basis. OD literature describes civility and incivility as unique to particular situations (Pearson et al. 2005). Similarly, civil behaviors in CREW are understood as culturally specific to each workplace; a rural Midwestern workgroup and a large urban Northeastern workgroup may each define civility differently. Variability in interpreting what constitutes civil behaviors is therefore intentional (conceptually driven) in the model. It reflects the reality of largely dissimilar content that characterizes interpersonal climate across organizations, and even across units within the same organizations participating in CREW. This distinction, loosely similar to differentiating between a construct and its operationalization in experimental research (e.g. "positive reinforcement" as a broad concept, versus "offering a candy bar" as a specific way to operationalize it), is crucial for understanding the CREW model.

CREW is thus a customized, initiative-based approach, based on the participants' experience of the workgroup process, and allowing each group to define its interpersonal norms (civil behaviors and attitudes), choose specific areas of focus, and agree on intervention processes to promote civility within their specific group. Local uniqueness, which cannot be fully captured by the large categories such as occupation, industry, or geographic region, serves as a defining context for designing, planning and implementing CREW interventions. The expectation of adapting every intervention to the locally appropriate understanding of civility is reflected within operational plans. Instead of attempting to standardize processes and techniques across participating sites, CREW operational plans emphasize adaptability of the intervention design, not only across participant groups (the intervention content is defined by local participants, not researchers or interventionists), but also across time (the content is redefined by the participants as needed, to the extent that the workplace culture changes through time as a result of the intervention itself).

The mechanism of change that theoretically explains positive change during CREW interventions is that, for the intervention period, organizations commit to giving time, attention, and support to having regular workgroup-level conversations about civility. These conversations create room for a dialogue that serves to bring civility-related aspects of organizational life to the collective awareness of the group. Putting these (group-specific) issues on the agenda and considering them together, in the shared interpersonal context of the group's work-life, provides group members regular opportunities for reflection and better understanding. More awareness and better understanding represent intermediate outcomes of the CREW process which support the subsequent work of group members identifying specific issues for a more focused discussion, giving these issues collective attention, and then devising actions to take.

This understanding of what causes change and how it unwraps reflects the client-centered roots of OD (Herzberg et al. 1959; Maslow 1973; Rogers 1977). The clients of CREW interventions are the workgroups, and the process that transpires in groups participating in CREW has to do with collective meaning-making. Given the inherent contextual dependence of this process (every workgroup is different and unique from others, in a way similar to individuals' personalities), the organizational client's motivation is considered to be the main driver of change, and participants own beliefs and perceptions (e.g., regarding what needs to be improved and what will constitute improvement) are taken as an optimal guide for direction. The organization provides conditions that facilitate change (time, attention and support for examining workplace climate.) The OD practitioner's role is to help clients clarify their current situation, needs, and motives and discover their capacity to make choices. The practitioner does this by supporting the client's focus on their own thinking and planning process; that is, the facilitator does not articulate the needs, define directions, or devise plans on behalf of the client. The practitioner's contribution to change is providing conditions for the client's own work, that is, making room (committing time, space, and resources to weekly discussions of workplace civility) and offering interpersonal support (positive attitude, sincere interest, active listening, ability to relate to the client's perceptions; cf. Rogers 1959). To summarize, much as in classic client-centered counseling (Bozarth 1999; Rogers 1959), the practitioner helps organizational clients design their own intervention and supports them as they carry it through.

To explicate the specifics of how CREW works, it is important to keep in mind that CREW is an intervention into the domain of organizational life that, by and large, is based on participants' psychological processes. Because of the interpersonal nature of the intervention focus (civility), OD practitioners who facilitate CREW as well as OD researchers who study it are bound to come in contact with "psychology's dual heritage" (Messer 2004): this refers to the coexisting scientific and humanistic traditions that both serve as sources of theories, concepts and methods for explaining and influencing human behavior. Like other professionals focused on changing behavior of individuals and groups (see Wampold 2007 for a discussion of psychotherapists), OD professionals often use the language and research tools created within medicine and science. However, they practice intervention procedures that rely on the same psychological processes and mechanisms within their clients as those processes that are involved in religious, spiritual, and culturally indigenous interventions. We suggest that accounting for CREW participants' psychological processes of meaning-making is of essence in clarifying how change happens in CREW.

Through our history as Homo sapiens, the human brain has evolved to develop an ability to make inferences about the internal states of others, particularly about their goals, desires, motivations, and beliefs (Boyer and Barrett (in press); Hutto 2004; Stich and Ravenscroft 1994; Wampold, 2007). This capacity to ascribe psychological meanings is deeply entrenched in our cognitive, affective and behavioral make-up, because it is evolutionarily adaptive. Meaning-making, and most specifically, interpretation of interpersonal cues enables us to predict the behavior of others, discriminate between predators and prey, get along, and create adaptive social groups (Wampold 2007). We also tend to form "coalitional alliances" (Boyer and Barrett in press) based on estimating other individuals' commitments to particular purposes, and develop friendships as safeguards against difficult times. Given the role these priorities have played in our survival as a species, meaning-making processes that support them are profoundly ingrained in our ways of assessing our environments, which, for a majority of contemporary Homo sapiens, includes their workplace. Whereas, in these authors' opinion, understanding how these processes operate is critical to explaining OD interventions in general, they have a particularly important role in explaining CREW because this intervention emphasizes a focus on relational (versus functional) aspects of organizational life.

Our account for how participants' meaning making during CREW interventions helps instill more civility is as follows. At the beginning of CREW, insofar as uncivil environments are concerned, participants' idiosyncratic explanations of what goes on in their workplace are often deeply involved in creating the very problems that plague the group. Perceptions of incivility from others motivate individuals to respond in kind, thus perpetuating more of similar behavior, to which other organizational members, in turn, respond in kind as well, and so forth (a phenomenon previously described as incivility spiral–Pearson et al. 2005) and civility spiral—Osatuke et al. 2009; Leiter et al. 2011). Making group members' perceptions of the interpersonal climate an explicit topic of discussion creates opportunities for participants to check themselves against others' perceptions, reevaluate their possibly inaccurate attributions, and learn how they themselves come across to others. Clearing any misinformed explanations about others, as well as becoming aware of one's own interpersonal impact, constitute mid-process outcomes in CREW. Accumulated over a series of CREW conversations that may cover multiple aspects of workplace interactions, these gains in shared understanding are intimately involved in altering how group members act towards each other at work.

Achieving improved (i.e. more accurate and detailed) interpersonal perceptions of coworkers' behaviors happens by means of a within-group dialogue of specific events and instances—those that the group members perceive as making impact on the interpersonal climate, and of which they all have an opinion through having witnessed them, or engaged in them, in their shared workplace. These instances provide a common ground of interpersonal knowledge; they serve as the shared referents for conversations during CREW, defining the "what" of a CREW intervention—its content, unique to each group. As group members exchange their perceptions of specific instances, individual meanings that they ascribe to them become known by others in the group, and other participants can react by sharing their own (convergent or divergent), meanings of the same referents. This creates a dialogical space whereby meanings that used to be individual and private become collectively known, making them subject to clarification, negotiation, and possibly, redefinition. This is a semiotically based process, fundamentally similar to the one that underlies creation of a language by ethnic, professional and cultural groups (see, e.g., Valsiner 2001; Vygotsky 1924/78). Through a shared experience in a shared environment, specific signs (e.g., terms, expressions, or behaviors) come to be reserved for expressing particular meanings, well understood by the in-groups. At the outcome, shared group norms are created which encompass meanings, signs that express them, and referent behaviors interpretable in terms of these signs and meanings. Importantly, this process involves more than sharing information through interpersonal communication (cf. Boyer 2001; Frank and Frank 1991); a CREW intervention is also an experience of co-creating and endorsing these norms. For example, participation in a CREW intervention cannot be substituted by didactic materials or a summary of new group norms regarding civility, even if these materials were customized to fit the needs of a particular group.

As a result of this process, to the extent that the workgroup did not experience particular problems with respect to civility, participants' achievements may include a greater repertoire of behaviors that express positive aspects of their shared workplace climate, along with the words to name those. For example, group members may find new ways of supporting and appreciating each other in the process of doing their work, as well as new ways of letting each other know about the support and appreciation. To the extent that the group had experienced interpersonal problems, the CREW process helps redefine these problems by explaining them in more accurate terms that reflect understandings checked with other members (including people who may be part of the problem). Redefining the problems is a prerequisite to formulating interpersonal concerns in addressable terms, reflecting more elaborate and accurate understandings of what goes into creating the problematic incidents. Independent of pre-intervention civility levels within participating groups, gains in collective understanding of what forms their civility climate heighten participants' ability to build upon positive climate aspects and resolve existing concerns in ways that maximize their collaboration and interpersonal well-being within their shared organizational environment and support them in advancing their shared (organizational) goals.

This view of the change process constitutes the rationale for the vast and intentional flexibility in CREW intervention design, positing it as a condition for success rather than as a limitation to be overcome (e.g. a lack of standardized intervention techniques or implementation processes). It also elevates participants' engagement in the process to a new level of importance, casting it among the main causal influences on the outcome. Participants' experience of, and involvement in, the organizational change process represent important, but typically understudied aspects in OD research (Bartunek et al. 2006). The importance that we attribute to contextually defined aspects of change parallels insights from empirical research acquired in fields other than OD but also interested in bettering people's interactional processes through applying interpersonally based interventions. For example, in counseling and psychotherapy research, aspects of relationship between treatment participants (alliance, empathy) have been extensively documented to make as much as, or more, difference for treatment outcomes than the specific treatments used (Norcross 2002; Wampold 2001; Ahn and Wampold 2001). Research in these fields also highlights the client's own contribution to change process, suggesting that it is important to study how clients actively transform what they receive for their own productive uses (e.g., Norcross and Wampold 2011; Bohart and Tallman 1999).

Theoretically, the tenet of flexibility and adaptability in the intervention content is a well-established premise within OD process consultation models (Reddy 1994; Reddy and Phillips 1992; Schein, 1990, 1999, 2006). In particular, contemporary approaches to OD (Greiner and Cummings 2004) recognize the importance of focusing on organizational culture and climate, and specifically acknowledge a need for customized interventions able to withstand adaptations to different organizational contexts as well as adjustments by users throughout the implementation process. Nevertheless, for pragmatic purposes, the specific models and examples of such interventions remain largely unavailable for use by consultants and organizations. In this context, the contribution of CREW is that it offers an intervention model ready to use by organizations interested in taking practical steps to promote positive, civil workplace climate.

The scope of innovation introduced in the OD field by the CREW approach is comparable to the huge impact caused in the 1950s by the advent of person-centered approaches, which redefined the philosophy of treatment and basic assumptions about how it works in the fields of counseling psychology, psychotherapy, individual and group coaching. The CREW model represents a dramatic change in intervention paradigm compared to the more structured, content-expert driven OD approaches. Much like person-centered vis-à-vis more traditional (psychoanalytic or cognitive-behavioral) models of psychotherapy, this client-centered OD model steps away from a prescriptive stance where a central role in the change process is reserved for an expert interventionist systematically interpreting or addressing symptoms one by one. Instead of examining single symptoms of workplace malfunction, the CREW model focuses on the interactional climate of a given workplace as the common source of its specific problems. Instead of instructing clients in correct meanings or behaviors as suggested by an expert outsider, CREW both pushes and radically empowers them to consider what systematically shapes their ways of relating to each other, recognize better options, and begin practicing these while collectively monitoring how this process goes and evaluating its day-to-day outcomes. This approach transfers expertise and power from the interventionist to the client, consistent with the notion of *empowerment* in CREW. The positive relation of CREW to multiple employee and organizational outcomes (Osatuke et al. 2009; Leiter et al. 2011) is, we believe, largely due to a relationship between civility and psychological safety, i.e., individuals' perception of consequences of interpersonal risks in their work environments (Edmondson 2004). Psychological safety in prior research has been connected to organizational effectiveness, through its dramatic effect on people's ability to non-defensively discuss and correct work-related errors (Edmondson 1996). CREW aims at restoring the participants' capacity to routinely assess interpersonal aspects of their workplace and directly discuss them with others in the spirit of respect and cooperation, striving to come up with mutually acceptable norms that subsequently guide behaviors at work. Once this capacity is in place (i.e. civility becomes the norm and civil behaviors are actively practiced in the organization), obstacles to discussing potentially interpersonally risky work-related issues are removed. That is, the large and positive impact of CREW on organizational outcomes likely operates through its beneficial impact on the psychological safety of the working environment.

The customized approach adopted by CREW supports local autonomy, increases adaptability, and, we believe, ultimately explains the success of CREW interventions. However, by its very uniqueness, it also represents unique challenges to interventionists and researchers. These challenges stem from the following key conceptual premises of the model. First, in order to be successful, an intervention that promotes civility has to be thoroughly grounded in the existing culture of a specific workplace. Second, the local culture is unique to every workplace just as personality is unique to every individual. Third, the elements defining this culture *can,* and in a successful intervention *will,* change through the duration of treatment (cf. Rogers 1959). Therefore, successful interventions in the CREW framework should be "responsive": they flexibly adjust to the changing contexts and new needs that emerge on a moment-to-moment basis, rather than "ballistic": fully planned and specified in advance, as prescribed by intervention theories or practice manuals (Stiles et al. 1998).

The importance of *responsiveness* over any specific intervention ingredients is supported by process-outcome research in other fields (e.g. counseling, psychotherapy). For example, it is not the amount of any specific ingredient per se that makes a difference for the outcome, but the delivery of the ingredient (such as clarifications, supportive statements, advice) exactly when, where and to whom it is helpful—that is, *in response* to the presenting needs that emerge from the intervention context. The same underlying reasons explain the established importance of common factors (most notably, relational factors, such as alliance and empathy) in influencing outcomes of interpersonally focused interventions, well over and above the effects of distinctions between any specific treatments or treatment elements (e.g. Ahn and Wampold 2001; Wampold 2007). Research into common factors has demonstrated that when interventionists in different approaches respond to their clients, they commonly take the clients' presenting needs into account over and above the divergent conceptual prescriptions specific to their respective approaches. Moreover, interventionists also modify their response to clients, to optimize the match between what is offered and how clients receive it, such that the differences between treatment approaches tend to decrease as the interventions progress. This is particularly true for effective interventions, which powerfully suggests the importance of responsiveness in defining effectiveness. A lack of overall differences in outcome between specific intervention types or intervention ingredients has been documented in OD research as well (e.g. Porras 1979). We interpret these findings to suggest a crucial importance of *responsiveness* in defining success of OD interventions. As interventions proceed, clients' needs and perceptions often change or become redefined–a well-established reality in the OD field (Armenakis and Zmud 1979; Golembiewski et al. 1976; Millsap and Hartog 1988). Acknowledging that the clients and their circumstances would change—in fact, *expecting* that they would, to the extent that the intervention is working—renders the preconceived design of an OD intervention less important than its ability to respond to the clients' changing needs. This expectation of flexibility also requires methods of process-outcome study that reflect participants' moment-by-moment responsiveness to each other and to the emerging context, in a way that randomized controlled designs (RCTs) and global intervention categories cannot.

For example, the basic requirements of placebo-controlled RCT groups in medicine (blinding and indistinguishability) are impossible to implement in trials of interpersonally based treatments (such as psychotherapy; see Baskin et al. 2003). This is because controls never resemble the active treatments, unless they truly incorporate the active treatment ingredients—in which case, they would *become* as opposed to *resemble* active treatment groups. Further, standardization, the golden standard for establishing validity of interventions in experimental research (e.g. in medicine), is based several assumptions: (a) elements of efficacious treatment are dissociable (as opposed to interconnected) and hence subject to dismantling; (b) the treatment can be dissociated from its context (unique characteristics of participants and settings); (c) these characteristics remain stable through treatment; and (d) most participants (in our case, participating workgroups) present with a single, well-delineated issue to be addressed in treatment. None of these assumptions hold true for contextually based interventions grounded in participants' experience of interpersonal aspects of their workplace.

Moreover, standardization efforts in the experimental research and treatment paradigm (e.g. in RCTs) usually invite some form of manualization, which serves multiple useful purposes: minimizing variability within experimental conditions, ensuring that all participants in the same condition across different sites receive the same treatment, allowing precise matching of intervention and control groups, and describing, for treatment and research consumers, the specific intervention that is being provided and evaluated. Manualization in this paradigm becomes a way to operationalize (i.e. clearly define in ways that can be reproduced by others) what exactly the examined treatment is—unlike in the CREW model that invites participants themselves to define what civility means to them, behaviorally.

From the experimental paradigm, the best intervention manual is one that standardizes the "dose," its timing, and its specific ingredients—specifying, for example, not only the number of treatment sessions but also precisely what should happen in each session, in which manner, and sequence (Westen et al. 2004). It follows (Westen et al. 2004) that manualization efforts succeed only insofar as they minimize clinical judgment and responsiveness to needs and problems that emerge during an intervention (as opposed to being planned in advance). In other words, standardization goals are limited by the extent to which interventions require a competent decision maker, one who, unlike the manual's authors, is present in the treatment situation and must decide how, when and where to intervene on the basis of understanding the principles of the intervention model, over and above their operationalization in the manual. Whether such decision-makers include interventionists, consultants, or clients themselves, the more they participate in defining, modifying, or adjusting what occurs during treatment compared to what is described in the manual, the less applicable the experimental methods become to understanding what makes the intervention work. Whenever the situational contingencies unwrapping during the intervention invite a response from consultants and participants, the exercise of judgment implicit to responding to this new information renders the treatment non-standard, as the procedures administered are no longer the exact procedures described in the manual. The experimental purity of treatment delivery is therefore reduced, the internal validity of treatment design is jeopardized, and it can no longer be concluded precisely which specific elements caused specific outcomes. In sum, standardization and manualization efforts, which are basic necessities within the experimental paradigm of designing and evaluating treatments, proceed from an assumption that the intervention is something done to the participants, rather than an interactive collaborative process that engages them (Westen et al. 2004)—an assumption fundamentally problematic for the CREW approach.

Importantly, the conceptual difference in defining how a treatment works and what makes it effective for contextually based models does not invite to relax the standards, either for intervention practice or for scientific quality of process-outcome research. Instead, this difference requires that the criteria of quality be different from those adopted in experimental research. For example, understanding how CREW interventions work requires a greater emphasis on convergent observation of events and processes in context, rather than on tightly controlling all variables except the manipulated ones, as typical in RCTs (cf. Greiner and Cummings 2004; Stiles 1993; Westen et al. 2004).

Like other fields interested in influencing human behavior in interpersonal context, OD professionals walk a "precarious epistemological tightrope" (Wampold 2007) in that they are often using the language of experimental laboratory to explain the culturally situated practices of meaning making. This may result in a tension between the subject matter and the methods used to explain how it works. Unless well-understood and balanced accordingly, the two paradigms (scientific and humanistic) create a potential for a "methodological war" (Rodgers and Hunter 1996). A typical "hardhead" question (Rodgers and Hunter 1996) is whether the intervention X, implemented using method Y, in the context of organization Z, succeeds or fails, and by what magnitude. A typical "softhead" question, in contrast, is asked from a practitioner's standpoint: what do I do now that works best for my organizational client, given their specific needs in this given moment? The first way of asking the question assumes that change components resemble boxes or bricks: elements which, when mechanically combined in a correct manner, make up a description of an intervention that is sufficient to describe and replicate it. The second way of asking the question focuses on a process occurring in real time, which is metaphorically more similar to a river rather than to a structure made of bricks. Tensions between two paradigms are typically created by attempts to use experimentally derived methods for characterizing process-oriented interventions—akin to explaining a river through a model designed for handling boxes.

To address the new research challenges created by unpredictability (flexibility and adaptability) of CREW intervention processes, we suggest that it may be helpful to lay aside RCT-inspired treatment models that liken contextually grounded OD interventions to medical treatments, and consider the meaning making that takes place within participating groups as a more promising focus of inquiry. This direction of study may move OD intervention researchers toward a more principle-oriented focus of inquiry, similar to the one taken by researchers in physics and biology, and away from a more mechanistic or applied focus typical of medical studies that collectively strive to generate an exhaustive list of which technique, applied by whom, to what kind of client, under which circumstances, causes what specific outcome. Examining the details of "how" change occurs in OD (based, for example, on enriched descriptions of the process from participants' and interventionists' standpoint) may become instrumental in understanding "why", thus offering a promise to clarify the mechanisms of change in interpersonal culture of organizations.

References

Adlerfer, C. P. (1972). *Existence, relatedness, and growth: Human needs in organizational settings*. New York: Free Press.

Ahn, H., & Wampold, B. E. (2001). Where oh where are the specific ingredients? A meta-analysis of component studies in counseling and psychotherapy. *Journal of Counseling Psychology, 48*, 251–257.

Anderson, L. M., & Pearson, C. M. (1999). Tit for tat? The spiraling effect of incivility in the workplace. *Academy of Management Review, 24*, 452–471.

Argyris, C. (1964). *Integrating the individual and the organization*. New York: Wiley.

Armenakis, A. A., & Zmud, R. W. (1979). Interpreting the measurement of change in organizational research. *Personnel Psychology, 32*, 709–723.

Bartunek, J. M., Rousseau, D. M., Rudolph, J. W., & DePalma, J. A. (2006). On the receiving end: Sensemaking, emotion, and assessments of an organizational change initiated by others. *The Journal of Applied Behavioral Science, 42*, 182–206.

Baskin, T. W., Tierney, S. C., Minami, T., & Wampold, B. E. (2003). Establishing specificity in psychotherapy: A meta-analysis of structural equivalence of placebo controls. *Journal of Consulting and Clinical Psychology, 71*, 973–979.

Bohart, A. C., & Tallman, K. (1999). *How clients make therapy work: The process of active self-healing*. Washington: APA Books.

Boyer, P. (2001). *Religion explained: The evolutionary origins of religious thought*. New York: Basic Books.

Boyer, P., & Barrett, H. C. (in press). Domain-specificity and intuitive ontology. In D. M. Buss (Ed.), *Evolutionary psychology handbook*. New York: Wiley.

Bozarth, J. D. (1999). *Person-centered therapy: A revolutionary paradigm*. Ross-On-Wye, UK: PCCS.

Edmondson, A. (1996). Learning from mistakes is easier said than done: Group and organizational influences on the detection and correction of human error. *Journal of Applied Behavioral Science, 32*, 2–28.

Edmondson, A. (2004). Psychological safety, trust, and learning in organizations: A group lens. In R. M. Kramer, R. M., Cook, K. S. (Eds.), *Trust and distrust in organizations: Dilemmas and approaches* (pp. 239–272). New York: Russell Sage.

Frank, J. D., & Frank, J. B. (1991). *Persuasion and healing: A comparative study of psychotherapy* (3rd ed.). Baltimore: Johns Hopkins University Press

Golembiewski, R., Billingsley, K., & Yeager, S. (1976). Measuring change and persistence in human affairs: Types of change generated by OD designs. *The Journal of Applied Behavioral Science, 12*, 133–157.

Greiner, L. E., & Cummings, T. G. (2004). Wanted: OD more alive than dead! *Journal of Applied Behavioral Science, 40*, 374–391.

Herzberg, F., Mausner, B., & Snyderman, B. B. (1959). *The motivation to work*. New York: John Wiley.

Hutto, D. D. (2004). *The limits of spectatorial folk psychology. Mind and Language, 19*, 548–573.
Laschinger, H. K. S., & Finegan, J. E. (2005). Using empowerment to build trust and respect in the workplace: A strategy for addressing the nursing shortage. *Nursing Economics, 23*, 6–13.
Leiter, M. P., Laschinger, H. K. S., Day, A., & Gilin-Oore, D. (2011). The impact of civility interventions on employee social behavior, distress, and attitudes. *Journal of Applied Psychology, 96*, 1258–1274.
Likert, R. L. (1961). *The human organization*. New York: McGraw-Hill.
Maslow, A. H. (1973). *Dominance, self-esteem, self-actualization: Germinal papers of A. H. Maslow*. New York: Brooks/Cole.
Messer, S. (2004). Evidence-based practice: Beyond empirically supported treatments. Professional Psychology: *Research and Practice, 35*, 580–588.
Millsap, R. E., & Hartog, S. B. (1988). Alpha, beta, and gamma change in evaluation research: A structural equation approach. *Journal of Applied Psychology, 73*, 574–584.
Norcross, J. C. (Ed.). (2002). *Psychotherapy relationships that work: Therapist contributions and responsiveness to patient needs*. New York: Oxford University Press.
Norcross, J. C., & Wampold, B. E. (2011). What works for whom: Tailoring psychotherapy to the person. *Journal of Clinical Psychology: In Session, 67*(2), 127–132.
Osatuke, K., Moore, S. C., Ward, C., Dyrenforth, S. R., & Belton, L. (2009). Civility, respect, engagement in the workforce (CREW): Nationwide organization development intervention at Veterans Health Administration. *The Journal of Applied Behavioral Science, 45*(3), 384–410. doi: 10.1177/0021886309335067i.
Ostroff, C. (1992). The relationship between satisfaction, attitudes, and performance: An organizational level analysis. *Journal of Applied Psychology, 77*, 963–974.
Parker, C. P., Baltes, B. B., Young, S. A., Huff, J. W., Altman, R. A., Lacost, H. A., et al. (2003). Relationships between psychological climate perceptions and work outcomes: A meta-analytic review. *Journal of Organizational Behavior, 24*, 389–416.
Pearson, C., Andersson, L., & Porath, C. (2005). Workplace incivility. In P. Spector & S. Fox (Eds.), *Counterproductive workplace behavior: Investigations of actors and targets* (pp. 256–309). Washington: American Psychological Association.
Porras, J. I. (1979). The comparative impact of different OD techniques and intervention intensities. *The Journal of Applied Behavioral Science, 15*, 156–178.
Reddy, W. B. (1994). *Intervention skills: Process consultation for small groups and teams*. San Diego: Pfeiffer.
Reddy, W. B., & Phillips, G. (1992). Traditional assessment: The way of the dinosaur. *OD Practitioner, 24*, 1–2.
Rodgers, R., & Hunter, J. E. (1996). The methodological war of the hardheads versus the softheads. *Journal of Applied Behavioral Sciences, 32*(2), 189–208.
Rogers, C. R. (1959). A theory of therapy, personality, and interpersonal relationships as developed in the client-centered framework. In S. Koch (Ed.), *Psychology: A study of science* (Vol. 3, pp. 184–256)., Formulation of the person and the social context New York: McGraw Hill.
Rogers, C. R. (1977). *Carl Rogers on personal power*. New York: Delacorte.
Schein, E. (1990). Organizational culture. *American Psychologist, 45*, 109–119.
Schein, E. (1999). *Process consultation revisited: Building the helping relationship*. Reading: Addison-Wesley-Longman.
Schein, E. (2006). Culture assessment as an OD intervention. In B. B. Jones & M. Brassel (Eds.), *The NTL handbook of organization development and change: Principles, practices, and perspectives* (pp. 456–465). San Francisco: Jossey-Bass.
Stich, S. P., & Ravenscroft, I. (1994). "What is folk psychology?", *Cognition, 50*, 447–468.
Stiles, W. B. (1993). Quality control in qualitative research. *Clinical Psychology Review, 13*, 593–618.
Stiles, W. B., Honos-Webb, L., & Surko, M. (1998). Responsiveness in psychotherapy. *Clinical Psychology: Science and Practice, 5*, 439–458.
The United States Postal Service Commission (2000). *Report of the U.S. Postal Service Commission on a Safe and Secure Workplace*. Prepared by the National Center on Addiction

and Substance Abuse at Columbia University: New York. Retrieved from http://purl.access.gpo.gov/GPO/LPS12068.

Valsiner, J. (2001). Process structure of semiotic mediation in human development. *Human Development, 44*, 84–97.

Vygotsky, L. S. (1924/78). *Mind and Society: The Development of Higher Psychological Processes.* Cambridge: Harvard University Press.

Wampold, B. E. (2001). *The great psychotherapy debate*. Mahwah: Erlbaum.

Wampold, Bruce E. (2007). Psychotherapy: The humanistic (and effective) treatment. *American Psychologist, 62*(8), 857–873.

Westen, D., Novotny, C. M., & Thompson-Brenner, H. (2004). The empirical status of empirically supported psychotherapies: Assumptions, findings, and reporting in controlled clinical trials. *Psychological Bulletin, 130*, 631–663.

Young, G. J. (2000). Managing organizational transformations: Lessons from the Veterans Healthcare Administration. *California Management Review, 43*, 66–82.

Chapter 6
The Impact of CREW

Abstract This chapter draws from a research program led by the author and colleagues to enhance the quality of workplace environments. It included an intervention study to evaluate the Civility, Respect, and Engagement at Work (CREW) intervention from the Veteran's Hospital Administration. This project applied a modified version of the process in five Canadian hospitals. The chapter explores the background research with reference to the Risk Management Model. The chapter ends by considering strategies for enduring improvements in workplace civility.

Evaluating CREW in Canadian Hospitals

A meeting of university researchers and chief nursing officers of Nova Scotia health districts explored possibilities for working together on action research. We were developing a proposal to the Partnerships in Health Services Improvement program (PHSI, pronounced fizzy) of the Canadian Institutes for Health Research (CIHR). The conversation ranged through leadership, burnout, and work engagement among other topics, but eventually reached a consensus on workplace incivility. Each of the health districts had problem units. Some units were toxic. These seriously problematic units had raised challenges for leadership for a long time. They had tried many strategies to address these problems, including imposing discipline on individuals with abusive behavior, transferring troublemakers elsewhere, and sending in new leadership. Although these actions would give temporary relief, they never produced enduring, satisfactory results.

We explored the literature on workplace mistreatment and found concern for alleviating the problem and calls for action to develop effective interventions. However, we found very few examples of systematic approaches to addressing the

M. Leiter, *Analyzing and Theorizing the Dynamics of the Workplace Incivility Crisis*, SpringerBriefs in Psychology,
DOI: 10.1007/978-94-007-5571-0_6,

problem. We could not find any examples of controlled quasi-experimental studies in organizations that had produced convincing evidence of any method's effectiveness. Finally, a member of our team connected with the team from the Veterans Health Administration (VHA) who are the authors of Chap. 5 in this book.

In the summer of 2008 with funding from CIHR and others we embarked upon our first round of CREW with eight units across five hospitals participating and another 33 units as a waiting list control. The major research report from that project (Leiter et al. 2011) reported a clear effect for CREW. Using Hierarchical Linear Modeling with intervention (CREW vs. Control) and Time (Before vs. After) as independent variables, the analysis found interaction effects for coworker civility, supervisor incivility, respect, cynicism, job satisfaction, management trust, and absences. Improvements in civility mediated improvements in attitudes.

Background

This research program provided support for key elements of the Risk Management Model. The research examined the quality of social exchanges among members of workgroups in five hospital settings. It assessed both ends of the social continuum: civility among colleagues as well as instances of incivility. It inquired about interactions with colleagues as well as interactions with supervisors. To balance these assessments of received social behavior, it also assessed participants' self-reports of incivility towards their colleagues. Together, the assessment produced an informative profile of each workgroup's social climate. Through a series of analyses we examined the connections of these social variables with employees' attitudes and perceptions about work.

Initially we established that incivility at work was a stressor in itself. Workplace mistreatment makes social contact among people at work an additional demand sapping employees' energy and enthusiasm rather than a resource for addressing the legitimate demands of a job. Following this logic an analysis established that nurses' perceptions of empowerment, supervisor incivility, and cynicism were strongly related to job satisfaction, organizational commitment, and turnover intentions (Laschinger et al. 2009). Incivility combined with burnout to be the most powerful predictors of turnover intention. Motivation to escape a workplace is consistent with nurses viewing it as a more risky environment in terms of their career aspirations as well as their well-being. Exhaustion augments employees' motivation to escape in that they lack the necessary energy resources to cope effectively with a more risky environment. Without effective coping resources, the environment appears even more hazardous. Cynicism aggravates the relationship with turnover in that it reflects a weaker attachment of employees to their job. The distancing reflected in the cynicism aspect of burnout describes psychological escape that often precedes the physical escape of absences and turnover.

The playing field for incivility at work is not level. GenX nurses report more incivility from colleagues than do their Baby Boomer colleagues (Leiter et al. 2010). Incivility occurs more readily across group boundaries. An in-group/out-group bias increases the probability of both intentional and unintentional incivility. This study found that the more junior and therefore lower status members of the workforce were more often recipients of incivility from their coworkers, adding to their demand level at work.

A structural equation analysis (Leiter et al. 2012) supported a job demand resources model of burnout and engagement in finding that incivility was related to the core burnout scales of exhaustion and cynicism while resources (i.e., civility) was related to professional efficacy and work engagement. This analysis reinforced the conception of working relationships residing on both sides of the demand and resource balance with the level of civility or incivility as a decisive indicator. The experience of incivility was related to later increases in exhaustion and cynicism. The analysis found that instigated incivility—employees' acknowledging that they behaved uncivilly towards their coworkers—was better predicted by low civility than by high levels of incivility. It appeared that the lack of a civil work environment reflecting a core value of respect was a more salient factor in employees behaving in an uncivil manner than was receiving incivility from others. This finding suggests that the core values of a workgroup are a more important issue than revenge or reciprocity in employees' social behavior.

A further analysis (Gilin-Oore et al. 2010) established that in addition to being a stressor in itself, incivility aggravates the relationships of other stressors on employee wellbeing. This analysis identified supervisor incivility as a moderator of the relationship of worklife qualities with employee well-being. First, the relationship of work overload with mental health was stronger for employees who encounter higher levels of coworker incivility. Similarly, the relationship of control with mental health was also stronger for employees who encounter more coworker incivility. This relationship was striking in that the difference was evident for employees who had experienced any coworker incivility at all in contrast to colleagues who reported no coworker incivility. A similar pattern was found for supervisor incivility: for employees who had encountered any supervisor incivility in the past year there was a stronger relationship of work overload with stress symptoms than for those who had experienced none. The pattern was once again evident for respect: those who experienced less respect at work had a stronger relationship of work overload and of control with mental health than did those who had a positive experience of respect at work.

Coworker and supervisor incivility reflect the negative end of workplace relationships while respect reflects the positive, constructive end of the continuum. The moderation demonstrated in this study suggests that relationship qualities are more than a unit of resource that is added or subtracted from the resource balance depending on whether they are on the negative or positive side of social exchange. Positive relationships, in addition to being resources, provide a means of making effective use of other resources that are available and to apply those resources to managing the demands that arise. For example, employees with good working relationships can develop shared strategies for managing workload. They can cover for one another, allowing individuals to rest or to manage child care during the working day. Those without respectful working relationships would lack important tactics for controlling the demands and time flows of their work days. Incivility creates barriers among colleagues, depriving them of the capacity to access one another's knowledge, emotional support, or energy to address demands. Overall, the workgroup becomes less effective because it lacks the means to coordinate its inherent resources to the best effect to provide treatment or to create products. In summary, a major message from this study is that collegial relationships function as an enabler for workgroups, allowing them to perform effectively with the demand/resource balance they experience.

One of the dynamics that perpetuate incivility among members of workgroups is the use of cognitive rationales. Although few people openly acknowledge a desire to treat their colleagues with disrespect, people readily generate excuses for their bad behavior. Leiter et al. (2010, August) identified three rationales that are used within workplaces. (1) The Pressure rationale acknowledges one's behavior was wrong and out of character, but blames incivility on the environment (in terms of feeling stressed or pressured by too much work, pressing deadlines or demands from other people. (2) The Toughness rationale reflects arguments that one's behavior is tough, but necessary, in that work context. For example, one must speak bluntly to inspire action from colleagues at work. By doing so, this toughness rationale may even make a virtue of uncivil behavior. (3) The Sensitivity rationale contends the behavior is not uncivil, but other people erroneously describe it to be so because these people are overly sensitive. This rationale denies incivility and puts the blame on other people over-reacting. In a sample of Canadian health care providers the sensitive rationale was endorsed most frequently, while the toughness rationale was endorsed less often, and the pressure rationale was reported least frequently. Despite differences in the use of each rationale, all three rationales moderated the relationship between experienced incivility and instigated incivility: those who used the rationales more frequently instigated incivility more readily in response to experienced incivility.

In hospitals, the working relationship of physicians and nurses has a compelling quality in defining the social environment. Galletta et al. (2012) found that nurses' evaluation of their working relationships with physicians moderated the association of affective commitment with turnover intentions. The moderating effect operated at the work unit level. The analysis defined for each hospital unit an average rating for nurse/physician relationship. In units with a positive rating, affective commitment—the enthusiasm nurses expressed towards their hospital—was more strongly related to their intention to stay than was the case in units with a poor rating of nurse/physician relationship. This pattern suggests that nurses' enthusiasm for their work has less consequence when they encounter incivility from physicians. By using hierarchical linear modeling (HLM) the analysis confirmed that the quality of the workgroup community had an impact distinct from that of individual encounters.

Bringing About Change

The Risk Management Model proposes (Proposition 4) that improvements in civility occur through a reflective process. Without reflection, the emotional tone of a workplace perpetuates itself through reciprocity and social contagion. Secondly, consistent with the Model's proposition that workgroup climate is self-perpetuating, we expected that interventions that target the workgroup level would have a more enduring impact. The overall respect and civility among members of a workgroup does not arise from a mass of independent individual decisions but from a network of inter-dependent events that build upon one another. One individual diligently attending to etiquette has the potential to improve that person's encounters. These efforts can make a worthy but limited improvement when taking the whole workgroup into consideration. These exchanges are unlikely to have a broad impact on the overall quality of the workplace environment.

A group of individuals working to conduct their interactions is more powerful. First, a group has a larger number of encounters with others within the workgroup. Through these encounters they have more opportunities to promote a more positive mode of social interaction. Second, group members can use their encounters with one another to develop both ends of a dialogue. For example, one individual assists another in a task; the assisted person expresses appreciation for the assistance; the assisting person receives the appreciation graciously. This exchange establishes more momentum than does an individual behaving well in the hope that someone may notice and respond accordingly. The cooperation occurring between the parties in the dialogue results in the exchange proceeding in an ideal fashion. Without cooperation, the exchange could break down: the assistance could be taken for granted with no expression of appreciation or the appreciation could be dismissed as improperly expressed. Instead, the cooperative exchange among group members aspiring to improve the civility in their workgroup reaffirms their efforts while producing a model for other workgroup members to follow.

As noted in Chap. 5, the active involvement of participants in defining the parameters of the intervention is an integral aspect of the intervention. Active participation engages the participants in (1) defining civility as it relates to their workgroup (2) adapting the intervention process to fit within their schedules and work area, and (3) make consequential decisions about specific activities and their timing within the overall intervention process. This level of participation would be much less intense in a highly structured intervention following a ballistic trajectory defined prior to implementation. These qualities help the developing standards for civility and respect to pervade the workgroup.

As with most workplace interventions, employees have some discretion about participation. Often this prerogative results in those who appear most in need of improving their behavior to avoid attending sessions. An intervention process that continues for six months in an active organization will fail to show perfect attendance of even the willing participants in light of travel commitments, absences, and vacations. As such, an effective intervention cannot rely entirely on the sessions alone to have an impact. Instead, the sessions provide a psychologically safe environment in which attendees can reflect on their behavior with the aim of exploring more fulfilling and respectful ways of interacting.

[Begin Box]

The CREW Process [In a Box to highlight this text]

What is CREW?

CREW is a series of structured gatherings among people who work together designed to enhance participants' sensitivity to the quality of their working relationship. CREW stands for Civility, Respect and Engagement at Work; the foundations to constructive and productive interactions amongst colleagues.

CREW Objectives

1. Participants become more sensitive to the impact of their social behavior on others.
2. Participants develop effective strategies for responding to incivility and disrespect at work.
3. Participants develop a deeper repertoire of supportive interactions with colleagues.

How Does It Work?

Organizational leaders, often with help from consultants, introduce CREW to the organization through town hall meetings, print media, and other formats. Through a series of discussions, leaders identify one or two work units to participate in the initial wave of the CREW process. A questionnaire survey assessing areas of worklife and workgroup social climate establishes a baseline assessment for participating units. Soon afterwards, CREW sessions are started. Once the sessions are finished a follow up assessment is done to measure the units' progress.

CREW Roles

Facilitators lead regular CREW sessions. A *Facilitator* draws upon a toolkit of conversational topics, information pieces, and structured group exercises to lead the CREW process on site. They:

- develop a plan for each session;
- gather any needed materials;
- inform participants of the session;
- communicate with the unit managers to ensure optimum participation with minimum disruption of the unit's work, and
- maintain ongoing updates with a member of senior management with a commitment to the initiative.

Unit Managers are integral to CREW's success. They work with *Facilitators* to ensure that the CREW sessions occur and that they fit within the life of the work of the unit without excessive disruption. They lead by example, by participating in the CREW sessions, and ensuring that the staff has an opportunity to attend. With help from the organization, the *Unit Manager* integrates the CREW process and philosophies into the everyday life of the unit, thereby ensuring sustainability.

Senior Management Champion keeps civility and respect high on the agenda for the organization. The Champions provide the primary link between the consultant and the organization. They:

- Champion CREW within the organization;
- Keep senior leadership informed of the CREW progress;
- Participate in the monthly CREW Community Conference Calls;
- Attend CREW Community meetings.

The CREW Process

CREW Preparation

1. Senior leadership endorses the CREW process as a strategy for realizing the organization's values regarding collegiality, respect, and teamwork.
2. The in-house expert or the consultant provides information sessions regarding CREW to stakeholders (board members, managers, EAP providers, leaders of labor or professional organizations).
3. Senior leadership tells the organization about CREW and its staged implementation and selects the initial units.
4. The in-house expert or the consultant provides information sessions to unit employees intending to participate in CREW.

Six Months of CREW

5. *Assessment.* A survey to establish a baseline. The survey results are compiled into a unit profile and may be used as a CREW session starting point.
6. *Facilitator Orientation.* Facilitators meet with the Champion and relevant Managers to become acquainted with matters of concern and opportunities that could help the CREW process. The Facilitator works out a process for managing the logistics of the CREW meetings.
7. *CREW Community Orientation.* The first CREW Community Events brings together Facilitators, Unit Managers, and CREW Champions. The day's events provide CREW background and training. Facilitators receive the Profile for their unit and begin their planning process in collaboration with their Coordinator, and Unit Manager.

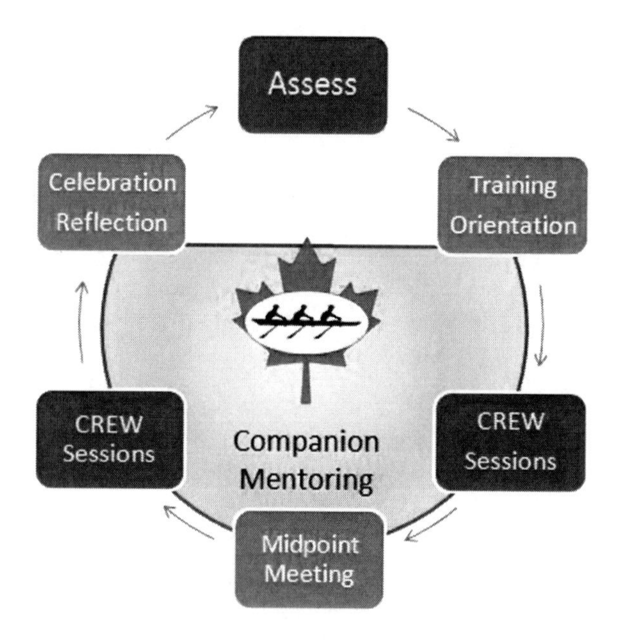

8. *Kickoff.* After the Orientation, the kickoff celebrates and launches CREW on the participating units. The kickoff is an upbeat, fun event but delivers a crucial message: it is an organizational priority, and allows potential participants to make an informed decision about their personal CREW participation.
9. *CREW Sessions.* CREW sessions occur through a six-month process of regular meetings. The baseline schedule for CREW sessions is one hour weekly. Groups adapt this standard to the pace of their work. One alternative is ten-minute meetings two or three times per week. During the sessions, facilitators introduce a topic or exercise. Initial sessions often start with icebreaker exercises from the Toolkit to get the conversation going. They continue to substantive exercises or discussion topics. An early substantive topic is: "How do we show support to one

another in this team?" A complementary question is: "What do we do when acting rude to one another?" Facilitators strive to encourage active participation in the dialog. They also ensure that individuals feel safe to express themselves in the sessions. As sessions progress, Facilitators encourage participants to take responsibility for the quality of their social environment at work, both by comporting themselves with civility and responding effectively to incivility when it occurs. The Survey Results Profile may be used to provide direction to facilitators in selecting information and exercises from the CREW Toolkit in the initial meetings.

10. *Second Assessment.* During the final weeks of the six-month process, members of the participating workgroups complete a second survey, identical to the first, with a few additional items reflecting on their experience with CREW. A second profile is generated providing an assessment of any changes.
11. *CREW Community Gathering.* Another CREW Community Event is the Midpoint. Facilitators, Coordinators, and Unit Managers attend a gathering led by the consultant. It is an opportunity to share frustrations, victories, problems, and solutions. The Midpoint shows a learning community in action.When a Gathering occurs towards the end of the six-month process, Facilitators receive the complete Profile summarizing responses from before and from after CREW. The Profile provides a take-off point for a critical evaluation of CREW's contribution. CREW units may present posters summarizing the history of their CREW experience. An important agenda item is identifying strategies for maintaining gains from CREW.

Conclusion and Follow-Up

1. *Sustainability Activities.* CREW never completely ends. The regular meetings and guidance from Champions draws to a close after six months, but the workgroup continues civility as a topic of reflection indefinitely. Civility and respect may become ongoing agenda items for team meetings with a member responsible for bringing a tip or lea a discussion on a related topic.
2. *First-line Managers.* The first-line manager of a work unit plays a pivotal role in sustaining the gains from the CREW process. By actively involving the manager throughout the CREW process from planning through implementation to follow-up, the process lays the groundwork for sustaining change. Ideally, the CREW process confirms the manager as a champion of a respectful work culture. Should the process identify that the manager lacks the commitment or skills to support a respectful workgroup culture, that gap requires action through coaching or other forms of professional development.
3. *Follow-Up Assessment.* A thorough process would conduct assessments annually to assess the development of the civility culture over time.

[End Box]

Implications of Improved Civility

The CREW process includes exercises and discussions that focus on the quality of relationships at work. For example, an initial exercise asks participants to respond to the question: What is civility for our group? How would we show civility towards one another in our workday? A companion exercise asks: How do we show disrespect toward one another? What are the actions and words that define uncivil behavior here? An honest and meaningful conversation on these topics requires a sense of psychological safety for the group and capable guidance from a facilitator. There is a risk that a group would give a superficial consideration to the questions. Participants may blame others for their problems. The finding that CREW affected employees' attitudes through improvements in civility (Leiter et al. 2011) confirms the compelling quality of personal relationships in the connections people make with their work.

Enduring Change

In a follow up to the CREW intervention reported in Leiter et al. (2011), the research team investigated the extent to which improvements found soon after competing CREW remain evident one year later (Leiter et al. in press). The analysis examined whether the results over time would follow one of three models: (1) *Steady State* in which the improvements achieved at Time 2 would remain in effect at Time 3 (2) *Augmentation* in which improvement would continue from Time 2 to Time 3, or (3) *Lost Momentum* in which the improvements at Time 2 would revert at Time 3 to Time 1 levels after the end of active intervention.

For workplace civility, incivility, and distress, the pattern followed an Augmentation model for the intervention groups in which improvements continued after the end of the intervention. For work attitudes, the pattern followed a Steady State model for the intervention group in that they sustained their gains during intervention, but did not continue to improve. For absences the pattern reflected a Lost Momentum model in that the gains from pre-intervention to post-intervention were lost, as absences returned to the pre-intervention level at follow-up.

These results are encouraging in that they provide evidence of CREW establishing fresh momentum in a positive direction. The improvement in both civility and incivility suggest that the workgroups who had participated in CREW had established social contagion in the right direction. The way that people interacted with one another was prompting positive spirals that improved the balance of civility to incivility over time.

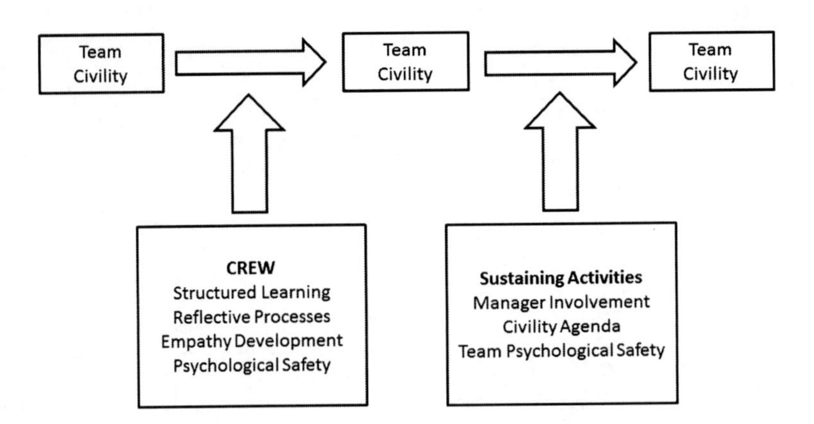

The diagram summarizes the CREW process, comprising structured learning, reflective processes, empathy development, and psychological safety, as having a moderating effect on the overall civility level of a team. When CREW occurs, that level improves; when CREW does not occur, that level remains constant. This moderation was confirmed in the research of both the Osatuke et al. (2009) study and the Leiter et al. (2011) study. The second moderating effect derives from sustaining activities, comprising manager involvement, keeping civility on the agenda, and maintaining psychological safety in the team's day-to-day operations. When these activities are present, a group is more likely to show a Steady State or even Augmentation model for its gains; when they are absent, the team is more likely to show a Lost Momentum pattern. This interaction has not yet been tested. The units involved in the Leiter et al. (in press) analysis reported engaging in the sustaining activities; they were not manipulated to test whether their absence would make a difference in their follow-up results.

Conclusion

The Enhancing Workplace Communities research project developed a range of ideas with a potential to improve organizations' capacity to address civility concerns among their employees. The approach considers workgroups rather than individuals as the primary target of intervention because social behavior is a collaborative enterprise, even when the workplace culture runs contrary to everyone's hopes. The message from the CREW intervention is that workgroups have the capacity to improve themselves when members work together. With concerted and sustained effort, they can establish positive dynamics that can sustain a civil, respectful, and engaging worklife.

References

Galletta, M., Portoghese, I., Battistelli, A., & Leiter, M. P. (2012). *Preventing nursing unit turnover: a multilevel analysis of nurses' intention*. Presentation at the 10th Conference of the European Association of Organizational Health Psychology. Zurich, Switzerland.

Gilin-Oore, D., LeBlanc, D., Day, A., Leiter, M. P., Laschinger, H. K. S., Price, S. L., Latimer, M. (2010). When respect deteriorates: Incivility as a moderator of the stressor-strain relationship among hospital workers. *Journal of Nursing Management, 18*, 878–888.

Laschinger, H. K. S., Leiter, M. P., Day, A., & Gilin-Oore, D. (2009). Workplace empowerment, incivility, and burnout: Impact on staff nurse recruitment and retention outcomes. *Journal of Nursing Management, 17*, 302–311.

Leiter, M. P., Day, A., Laschinger, H. K. S., & Gilin-Oore, D. (in press). Getting better and staying better: Assessing civility, incivility, distress, and job attitudes one year after a civility intervention. *Journal of Occupational Health Psychology*.

Leiter, M. P., Laschinger, H. K. S., Day, A., & Gilin-Oore, D. (August, 2010). *Rudeness rationales: Whatever were they thinking*? Presentation at the Annual Conference of the Academy of Management. Montreal, Canada.

Leiter, M. P., Laschinger, H. K. S., Day, A., & Gilin-Oore, D. (2011). The impact of civility interventions on employee social behavior, distress, and attitudes. *Journal of Applied Psychology, 96*, 1258–1274.

Leiter, M. P., Nicholson, R., Patterson, A., & Laschinger, H. K. S. (2012). Incivility, burnout, and work engagement. *Ciencia & Trabajo*. (Science and Work), *14*, 22–29.

Osatuke, K., Mohr, D., Ward, C., Moore, S. C., Dyrenforth, S., & Belton, L. (2009). Civility, respect, engagement in the workforce (CREW): Nationwide organization development intervention at Veterans Health Administration. *Journal of Applied Behavioral Science, 45*, 384–410.

Chapter 7
Conclusion

Abstract This final chapter reviews the key constructs of the Risk Management Model. It proposes elements of a research agenda to address major outstanding issues in the field. Revisiting the major propositions of the model summarize a comprehensive perspective on workplace mistreatment and on interventions to address the problem.

Conclusion and Future Directions

The following propositions have guided the discussion of workplace mistreatment. They concern the emotional impact of problematic interactions, their persistence in work environments, and directions for initiating improvement in workplace cultures.

Proposition	Issue
Proposition 1: People want to belong: People are motivated to have good standing within a social group	The importance of civility and incivility at work Why mistreatment creates so much distress Why civil working relationships enhance wellbeing and productivity
Proposition 2: People notice: People have refined perception of social cues and a capacity to make sense of social situations	The powerful impact of subtle social cues Why civility is a ubiquitous dimension of worklife
Proposition 3: Workgroup climates are self-perpetuating	Why toxic work environments persist Why change strategies require sustained, structured procedures How reciprocity and social contagion sustain the status quo

(continued)

M. Leiter, *Analyzing and Theorizing the Dynamics of the Workplace Incivility Crisis*, SpringerBriefs in Psychology,
DOI: 10.1007/978-94-007-5571-0_7, © The Author(s) 2013

(continued)

Proposition	Issue
Proposition 4: Improving civility requires a reflective process	How to interrupt a social dynamic with momentum to sustain itself The importance of skilled facilitation in changing a workplace culture The shifts in perspective in individuals that facilitate change
Proposition 5: Improving civility benefits from (and promotes) psychological safety	Creating a distinct setting to encourage a reflective process Defining a key dimension of workplace culture to sustain civility

The Risk Management Model of workplace civility integrates work from a variety of perspectives to address outstanding issues in research on social relationships at work. Its core constructs pertain to important concerning challenges in improving the level of civility and respect in work environments.

The book begins by considering the importance of social relationships to explain both the emotional impact of incivility along with the capacity of people to interpret subtle social cues. The model builds upon a need for belong as a primary motive for behavior in response to incivility. It explains the intensity of emotional responses to incivility in that the implicit exclusion from a workplace community thwarts a fundamental human need.

The symbolic quality of incivility helps to explain the intense reactions in responses to low intensity forms of incivility. A major contribution of the incivility construct is that by assessing low intensity behavior of ambiguous intent it has broadened the focus to encompass mistreatment that occurs much more frequently than the high intensity behaviors associated with aggression and abuse. Despite its low intensity, as the Hershcovis (2011) analysis suggests, incivility has as great if not greater associations with distressful experiences. A statistical solution for incivility's power is that with fewer zero values in survey responses, correlations of incivility with other measures are more evident than would be correlations with the much less frequent events of abuse and aggression. An encouraging note is that even when assessing the low intensity behaviors within a modified version of the Workplace Incivility Scale in a study by my research group (Leiter et al. 2011), a significant proportion of the sample (39.6 % of 2904 responses) reported zero instances of supervisor incivility over the past year, 25.7 % zero coworker incivility, and 24 % zero instigated incivility. Although a majority still reported some incivility, the experience is not universal.

These considerations lay the foundation for appreciating the importance of civility in worklife. A basic need for belonging combined with practical benefits of maintaining social standing within a workgroup creates a compelling combination. Regardless of whether colleagues are behaving exceptionally badly or individuals have developed refined standards for social behavior, a gap between what one expects and what one receives in social discourse results in a strain. Finding a sustainable alignment of expectations and behavior becomes the objective.

Emphasizing the Workgroup

The Risk Management Model considers incivility as primarily a quality of the workgroup. Although acknowledging the existence of individuals with serious psychopathology within the workplace, the approach takes the position that enduring problems of workplace incivility reflect a workgroup or organizational problem. First, a worksetting that permits a dysfunctional individual to abuse colleagues lacks policies, procedures, and values appropriate to contemporary organizations. Second, the model proposes that most acts of incivility are perpetrated by normal people with good intentions. People mistreat others through thoughtlessness, short-sightedness, stress, or participation in unprofessional social dynamics. Anyone is capable of behaving badly; the defining issue is how frequently they behave badly. Our survey data noted previously found that coworker incivility—the most frequent of the three WIS subscales—two-thirds of the respondents had an average score less than one (a few times per year or less) and 90 % had scores less than two (once a month or less). Yet these low frequencies are associated with increased reports of distress compared to those with no experiences of incivility. The model proposes that the enduring impact of incivility reflects its symbolic power to define a hazardous work environment beyond the trauma associated with the unpleasant social exchange.

The social dynamics among colleagues demonstrate the values-in-action that may or may not be consistent with the espoused values of a workgroup. In the early twenty-first century workgroups espouse lofty values regarding teamwork, respect, and engagement. The growing gap between standards of respect and actual behavior may reflect an increasingly refined sense of fairness, civility, and respect. Historical documents and fictional accounts, such as the Mad Men TV series do not reflect a more respectful workplace in the past. One can find little convincing evidence of good old days. The more refined standards of etiquette for which some express nostalgia were generally limited to members of one's in-group with blatant expressions of racism and sexism at work. At present people are held to more demanding standards of comportment and are required to apply these standards universally, not simply to their friends. Organizational policies and legal sanctions back up standards of behavior. In short, both increased standards of comportment may partly explain the civility gap; it may not simply be a function of worsening behavior.

A Reflective Process

The Risk Management Model proposes a reflective process as the most effective means of improving the quality of a workgroup's culture. In contrast to reciprocity and emotional contagion that perpetuate the current state of affairs—for better or worse—a reflective process offers an opportunity for higher order cognitive processes to shape reactions to social behavior. On an individual level, empathy provides a means of breaking a spiral of incivility. A greater understanding of another person's perspective and feelings encourages a more generous response. The process of discovering another person's perspective through a meaningful conversation can be enlightening while encouraging a more trusting relationship between two people.

The CREW process explored through Chaps. 5 and 6 described a group-level reflective process. The exercises in the CREW *Toolkit* encourage members of workgroups to reflect together on the quality of their working relationships. By conversing about the ways in which they characteristically show respect or disrespect to one another, participants defuse the emotional charge that accompanies workplace mistreatment. The approach encourages a problem-solving perspective among the participants as they devise creative solutions to their challenges. In the course of role playing new, more civil ways of interacting with one another, they move social reactions into more rational parts of their minds. Rather than being driven by an irresistible, inevitable emotional reaction to others' behavior, their own social behavior becomes a more rational, practical event.

Psychological Safety

The contrast to feeling at risk is a sense of psychological safety. The trust upon which psychological safety depends comes about through a process, such as CREW, of working with people. The approach acknowledges that social relationships do present risks. People can experience harm or loss within a workgroup when working relationships go badly. One cannot in good conscience encourage a trusting attitude to the world in general. Trust is created and earned through meaningful exchanges among people who come to share core values along with a commitment to pursue those values in concrete ways.

The power of psychological safety is that it encourages learning by broadening one's perspective and facilitating the building of new capabilities (Fredrickson 2001). The model considers social behavior as learned behavior that is reinforced by a workgroup's values. Not only are people adept at interpreting the messages implicit in the behavior of those around them, they can readily adapt their behavior to align with the core values of their group. This quality can proceed smoothly when one shares the values of a group; it can be a strained process when those values contrast with personal values. The hope is that through cooperative effort people can bring about a workplace culture that is meaningful, fulfilling, and productive.

Future Research

The focus within this book has been on the risks inherent in uncivil work environments. The primary problem for workplace incivility occurs when mistreatment moves beyond the idiosyncratic behavior of a few individuals to become an intrinsic part of a workplace culture.

Initiating Incivility

The processes of reciprocity and social contagion help bad behavior resonate throughout a work environment, but they do not explain the initial appearance of incivility within a work environment. Initiating mistreatment in the workplace appears counterintuitive on the surface in that it has the potential to increase risk. The target of mistreatment may respond or authorities in the workplace may reprimand the instigator for proscribed behavior. One possible explanation is that instigators do not perceive risks because of their secure position. Some forms of mistreatment, such as bullying, are generally attributed to people who hold power by virtue of their hierarchical position, social connections, or physical strength. Complementing this dynamic may be that instigators have such disdain for their targets that they dismiss risks arising from them.

People may feel rewarded for showing incivility. Within a clique, showing disrespect towards out-group members may prompt supportive reactions from friends. This behavior could increase one's standing within a power-based group. Intimidating coworkers, especially junior members, may help to assure access to rewards, such as promotions or perqs. A full picture of the dynamics of instigating incivility would encompass the motivations of individuals as well as the policies and practices that tolerate or even encourage bad behavior.

Another potential dynamic is that employees who feel at risk are more likely to instigate workplace mistreatment towards others. The positive correlation of cynicism with instigated incivility (Leiter et al. 2011), consistent with the long standing connection of job burnout with poor working relationships (Maslach et al. 2001) are consistent with the proposition that experienced stress could prompt mistreatment towards colleagues. The cynicism construct reflects a distant, manipulative psychological connection with work that would be reflected in poor working relationships.

The instigated incivility variation of the Workplace Incivility Scale (WIS; Cortina et al. 2001) has provided a general perspective on employees' acknowledgement of rude behavior as has the Rudeness Rationales Scale (Leiter et al. 2010, August). Using these measures with more in depth assessments through interviews or diary studies could add greater depth to the relationships identified to date.

Another research priority is measurement development. Our research team has developed a new measure, the Straightforward Incivility Scale, with five items are quite general (e. g., "Spoke rudely to you"). Rather than attempt to adumbrate the vast array of ways in which people may act rudely to one another, the measure simply asks about general types of rudeness. We hope that this measure will be more useful in cross-cultural studies in which the question is the frequency with which people feel offended rather than the specific form of the rude behavior. Another measurement issue is that the current practice assesses civility in general terms that reflect the social climate of a workgroup while it assesses incivility as the frequency of discrete events. Exploring measures that have a more parallel structure may generate new insights into the social dynamics of workgroups.

Interventions

As noted elsewhere, books and websites provide advice for managing mistreatment at work. There is advice on ways for individuals to react constructively as well as direction for organizational policies and procedures. Efforts are underway to translate some of these concepts into legislation. Very little of this advice has received critical scrutiny. The advice generally makes sense, but it has not been evaluated for effectiveness or for its potential to generate unanticipated consequences that could prompt further problems for individuals or workgroups. At the least, people would benefit from dispensers of advice providing information on the research support for their approaches. A much better development would be cooperation with researchers to evaluate these approaches critically.

In Chap. 6 Osatuke and colleagues reflects on basic challenges in evaluating interventions in organizational settings. The model of contrasting intervention with control groups over time remains a viable model. The field would benefit from much more research following this model. Too much knowledge at present rests upon correlational analyses of questionnaires. The Randomized Clinical Trial (RCT) format does not transfer readily from evaluating medications to evaluating organizational procedures. It is not feasible to keep members of treatment control groups completely unaware of the larger research context. Active participation in the research project is an integral part of organization's participation in a project. By conducting multiple tests across diverse settings, a larger scale project can compensate for these limitations. Despite necessary departures from pure experimental designs, quasi-experimental research projects would make contributions that would be much more valuable than those generated by correlational survey analysis.

Conclusion

Workplace incivility raises serious concerns. In one dynamic, increasing standards for respectful treatment collide with relaxing standards of comportment. In another dynamic, an increasingly diverse global workforce encounters challenges people to appreciate new and diverse ways of expressing respect and appreciation. In a third dynamic, individuals gain positions of power without developing the sensitivity and perspective to use power graciously.

At the point of this writing, the research literature has established that incivility, abuse, bullying, mobbing, and other forms of mistreatment create distress and hurt performance. The state of knowledge remains much less clear on identifying the conditions that encourage people to mistreat their colleagues. There is only the beginnings of efforts to evaluated critically approaches to improve civility within a workgroup. The existing knowledge on impact has been the most available knowledge. Understanding the dynamics of perpetrating mistreatment and alleviating the problem present much greater challenges. Addressing the conditions that promote incivility is a challenge well worth the effort.

References

Cortina, L. M., Magley, V. J., Williams, J. H., & Langhout, R. D. (2001). Incivility in the workplace: Incidence and impact. *Journal of Occupational Health Psychology, 6*, 64–80.

Fredrickson, B. L. (2001). The role of positive emotions in positive psychology: The broaden-and-build theory of positive emotions. *American Psychologist, 56*, 218–226.

Hershcovis, M. S. (2011). Incivility, social undermining, bullying… oh my!: A call to reconcile constructs within workplace aggression research. *Journal of Organizational Behavior, 32*, 499–519.

Leiter, M. P., Laschinger, H. K. S., Day, A., & Gilin-Oore, D. (August, 2010). *Rudeness rationales: Whatever were they thinking*? Presentation at the Annual Conference of the Academy of Management. Montreal, Canada.

Leiter, M. P., Laschinger, H. K. S., Day, A., & Gilin-Oore, D. (2011). The impact of civility interventions on employee social behavior, distress, and attitudes. *Journal of Applied Psychology, 96*(6), 1258–1274.

Maslach, C., Schaufeli, W. B., & Leiter, M. P. (2001). Job burnout. *Annual Review of Psychology, 52*, 397–422.

Printed by Publishers' Graphics LLC